Notting Hill Editions is an independent British publisher. The company was founded by Tom Kremer (1930–2017), champion of innovation and the man responsible for popularising the Rubik's Cube.

After a successful business career in toy invention Tom decided, at the age of eighty, to fulfil his passion for literature. In a fast-moving digital world Tom's aim was to revive the art of the essay, and to create exceptionally beautiful books that would be lingered over and cherished.

Hailed as 'the shape of things to come', the family-run press brings to print the most surprising thinkers of past and present. In an era of information-overload, these collectible pocket-size books distil ideas that linger in the mind.

nottinghilleditions.com

Anouchka Grose is a psychoanalyst and writer practising in London and she is a member of The Centre for Freudian Research, where she regularly lectures. Her non-fiction books include *No More Silly Love Songs: A Realist's Guide to Romance* and *A Guide to Eco-Anxiety: How to Protect the Planet and Your Mental Health*, and her journalism and fiction have appeared in the *Guardian*, the *Independent* and *Granta*. She is also extremely fashionable.

FASHION

A Manifesto

–

Anouchka Grose

nh   Notting Hill Editions

Published in 2023
by Notting Hill Editions Ltd
Mirefoot, Burneside, Kendal, Cumbria LA8 9AB

Series design by FLOK Design, Berlin, Germany
Cover design: Tom Etherington
Creative Advisor: Dennis PAPHITIS

Typeset by CB Editions, London
Printed and bound by Memminger MedienCentrum,
Memmingen, Germany

Cover photograph © Michèle Côté

Make-up by Anna Inglis Hall
Hair by Tracey Cahoon
Stylist: Polly Banks
Photo Assistant: Hannah Burton

A CIP record for this book is available from the British Library.

ISBN 978-1-912559-49-7

nottinghilleditions.com

For Ali Rowe,
who fights so hard to make a better world

Contents

– Introduction –
1

– What is Fashion? –
9

– Status: How Clothes Position Us Socially –
21

– Fashion as Art –
34

– Horror: The Body in Fashion –
51

– Harm: How Our Clothes Can Hurt Us –
61

– Beauty and Ugliness: Fashion as Unlikely
Redeemer –
72

– Time: Why We Like to Wear the Same Stuff
at the Same Time –
87

– Technology: Are Digital Garments
the Answer? –
94

– Lucky Punk –
108

– Fashion's Alternative Future –
123

– Acknowledgements –
136

— Introduction —

I t feels a little anachronistic to be writing about fashion right now. We're still relatively fresh from pyjama-wearing lockdowns, and the Intergovernmental Panel on Climate Change has warned that we've already passed a number of environmental tipping points that pretty much guarantee we're on course to disaster. The idea that we should go out and buy clothes we don't need, to impress people who probably don't care, makes little sense. The clothing industry accounts for 10 per cent of the world's carbon emissions, while flying contributes a mere 2.4 per cent. Clothing production is also responsible for 20 per cent of the world's wastewater, not to mention widespread labour rights abuses, plus its part in industrial farming for the production of wool and leather. As people often like to point out these days, a T-shirt that costs £3.00 comes with untold costs for the planet. So by far the most sensible thing to say about fashion is simply: 'stop!'

Still, many of us remember the days when the seasonal influx of new shapes, colours and textures into the luminous paradises of H&M, Topshop and Miss Selfridge seemed a cause for celebration and joy. Like children who grew up eating chops only to discover that their favourite supper was hacked from the corpse of a fluffy lamb, we have somehow to metabolise the cognitive dissonance produced by the realisation that, all along, we've been funding a toxic regime. We understood that fashion was a bit scoundrelly from the way it knew how to prey on our insecurities in order to make us part with our cash. We were aware of the part it played in the proliferation of eating disorders. We'd clocked that reading *Vogue* often made us temporarily depressed. We'd seen *Zoolander* and *The Devil Wears Prada* and basically agreed that fashiony people can be idiots. But perhaps we didn't realise how enthusiastically it was ushering us headlong towards the apocalypse.

One small sign of hope is that the fashion industry itself now knows that we know that things can't go on this way. Heightened awareness of the severity of the climate crisis, plus the body positivity movement, plus an insistence on diversity that goes beyond tokenism all mean you can't keep pumping out images of skinny, white women in all-new swag and expect people to like you. Fashion, in the old sense, has become desperately uncool. Into this new space we're seeing a flood of upcycling, the use of reclaimed deadstock and an army of widely divergent bodies and faces. But is that enough to save fashion from the obsolescence it probably deserves?

Maybe not. But . . . I LOVE fashion and can't help

wishing that something of its ways could have a place in the future. The paradox of preserving an imaginary space in a future jeopardised by the very thing you're trying to save is hard to justify, but perhaps that can be the improbable purpose of this book. In order to get there, we can skip through the history of fashion and see what industrial and psychological forces caused it to take its present shape. We can look at the ways in which clothes, and changes of style, can help us to inhabit our bodies; and at fashion as a very particular art form, with its wonky combination of 'genius creators', mass production and unpredictable crowd behaviours. We will consider beauty, harm, technology and time as factors at work in the proliferation of new sartorial ideas, and ultimately argue for the possibility of fashion as an anarchic, hyper-social force for good. Or at least to put forward a new kind of fashion logic, purged of its traditional capacity for evil.

I feel I should declare my fashion credentials up front as they far from qualify me for rewriting the entire system. I spent many evenings growing up watching my mother dressing up to go out. I never wanted her to leave and would lounge around on her bed, extracting whatever enjoyment I could from her transitory presence. She was a journalist and fierce lunchtime shopper, always coming home with freshly-purchased, spangled, printed dresses, huge geometric earrings and colourful shoes – not to mention some quite experimental haircuts. Observing her, I made the link between exciting clothes and an exciting life: outfits like that demanded commensurate outings. If you wore amazing clothes, your life had to match them.

At the age of fourteen I decided that my life urgently needed to become more exciting, but my pocket money didn't go far in Chelsea Girl. I learnt to use a sewing machine, follow patterns, and scavenge for scraps of material in the laundry cupboard. My experimental wardrobe, made from dyed sheets and curtains – intercut with the odd charity shop find – meant I could become a hair model for Antenna, Boy George's hairdresser, which in turn meant I could hang out with other weirdly dressed people and even occasionally get into nightclubs. Thanks to clothes, my life finally began.

Since then my wardrobe has always been a mixture of home-made, second-hand and whatever I could afford from the Vivienne Westwood sale. Not to mention the odd H&M splurge. After going to art school and realising that it didn't qualify me for anything, I offered myself to the super-stylist, Katie Grand, as an intern. Amazingly, she said yes, but then another job got in the way. I've also visited the upper floors of Vogue House to be vetted for their subs desk. (My interviewer visibly scribbled encouraging comments on the form, then I never heard from her again.) I've written the occasional article for fashion magazines, done webcasts with influencers and presented papers about fashion at psychoanalytic conferences. I've always bought and sold vintage clothing, and had a stall in Portobello in the 90s. I can make a bra and pants from scratch. I'm hardly Grace Coddington, but I've done my time.

I became interested in fashion in a more theoretical sense at art school in the 90s, where we were encouraged to read psychoanalysis and critical theory. There were people, like turn-of-the-twentieth-century sociologist Thorstein Veblen, who treated fashion as an added extra that could be subtracted from our lives without any of us noticing that anything was missing. But then there were others, like the nineteenth-century French literary hero, Charles Baudelaire, who saw fashion as being inextricable from the rest of modern culture. I was amazed to discover that Freud and Lacan were both major fashion hags, and also that they made fascinating comments about clothing here and there in their work. Then there was Roland Barthes's mind-bending *The Fashion System* (1967), a semiotic study of the verbal and visual languages of fashion. Barthes explains that fashion is a language in which each garment is a word – in that its relation to meaning is arbitrary. But above all there was J. C. Flügel's seminal book *The Psychology of Clothes* (1930) which was almost impossible to borrow from the Goldsmiths' Library because it was always on loan to the legendary make-up artist Phyllis Cohen, who was studying fine art at the time. Flügel's book is cited in almost all subsequent books about the history, psychology or even sociology of fashion. It's amazing. And also, in places, amazingly wrong. His brilliant initial thesis is that clothing is like a neurotic symptom in that it tries to satisfy our wishes both to reveal and to conceal. Clothes are 'a blush on the face of humanity'; like a blush, they are a very visible sign of something one might wish to hide. So far so astute. However, by the end of the book, Flügel suggests that by the close of the twentieth century psychoanalysis will have had such a transformative effect on humanity that we will walk around naked, with strap-on wallets for our keys and money.

One of the many great things about Flügel's book is that it somehow manages to be a seminal masterpiece at the same time as being chronically misguided. In that sense it's the perfect inspirational text for someone barely qualified to embark on a set of speculations about the future of fashion. It's possible, as a complete outsider, to hurl out a load of ideas, have some of them heartily disproven and still not look like a complete idiot. Who knew? (Oh, did I mention, he also has a passing interest in eugenics?!)

There's also Edmund Bergler's awful *Fashion and the Unconscious*, from 1953, where he develops the idea of a 'fantastic fashion hoax' whereby gay male fashion designers take out their vicious unconscious impulses on women by making them wear uncomfortable and stupid-looking clothes. What's more, Bergler claims he can cure them of being gay without curing them of being fashion designers. Probably the less said about that one the better, although people still sometimes dutifully quote him in texts about fashion psychology.

The question it would be helpful to answer here is this: If we finally agreed to stop generating desire for unnecessary clothing on a mass scale, what would be left of fashion? Is that all fashion *is*? I think not, although it's certainly a major factor in the whole scheme. Without trying to answer the question too quickly, I can perhaps at least start by saying that I will try to stand up for fashion's less destructive qualities. The reason I will do this is that I am an addict who has no desire to give up her addiction. While I may consciously be aware that fashion is one of the many ways in which capitalism taps into our unconscious drives and desires in order to keep us enslaved, I'm also hooked enough to find it hard to imagine a life in which the satisfactions afforded by my addiction are no longer an option. At least we can say I'm a standard representative of my culture. I basically know it's game over, but there are some bits I'm desperate to hang onto. And didn't Marx suggest that we would keep many of the fruits of capitalism after the revolution?

Even today I'm torn between sitting at home writing this and jumping on my bike to head over to Oxford Street to look at a dress I saw in a shop window last night. Couldn't I just try it on? It was a knitted burgundy number with an unlikely turquoise and cream intarsia blob wafting across the midriff. It was kind of like the sweater dresses we wore in the 90s, but also satisfyingly futuristic. The shop was a new, terrible emporium offering fast turnover and a sickening quantity of choices, all cheaply made in super-destructive fibres and undoubtedly exploitative conditions; the kind of shop we know we mustn't shop in. Still, the dress managed to exert the kind of fascination that made me want to forget everything I know and to rush out and buy it. Surely I was allowed just this one infringement? That's how powerful fashion can be; it can override your moral compass – even when you're trying to write about the morality of fashion.

The fact that these words are here at all is testament to the fact that I didn't go to Oxford Street but instead committed to sitting down to begin to explore the problem.

– What is Fashion? –

Fashion, we have been brought up to believe (and generations of writers in a myriad of journals have contributed to this belief) is a mysterious goddess, whose decrees it is our duty to obey rather than to understand; for indeed, it is implied, these decrees transcend all ordinary human understanding. We know not why they are made, or how long they will endure, but only that they must be followed; and that the quicker the obedience the greater is the merit.

– J. C. Flügel, *The Psychology of Clothes*

Definitions of fashion tend to veer from the historical to the psychological to the sanctimonious. For some, 'fashion' has simply existed throughout human history. From the hot, woolly skirts of the Ancient Sumerians to the 2010s ubiquitous Kardashian beige, humans appear to exhibit a tendency to dress alike. This explains, in part, why a totally 'unfashionable' 1970s dad (ploofy moustache, corduroy trousers, knitwear) looks completely different from a determinedly normie contemporary one (unbuttoned shirt over T-shirt, nondescript jeans, deck shoes). While both dads might claim to have no interest in fashion, they are nonetheless dressed in the garments of their era.

The most orthodox theory of fashion, attributed to the British philosopher, sociologist and psychologist, Herbert Spencer, and repeated ad nauseam by fashion writers ever since, tells us that fashion as we now understand it was born out of the death of the European feudal system. Throughout the industrial revolution, as servants and farm labourers bought their freedom from impoverished aristocrats and moved to cities to set up their own businesses, the aristocracy began to worry about losing its power. On witnessing the newly formed bourgeoisie's growing affluence, aristocrats felt they had to re-establish the distinction between themselves and the rest of society. One of their more desperate strategies was the introduction of sumptuary laws, which forbade the middle classes from wearing the same clothes as them. These laws proved almost impossible to enforce – it can't have been easy to decide how different was different enough – so the aristocrats gave up on the idea of getting what they wanted through legislation and adopted another strategy of radically altering their mode of dress at moments when it seemed like the lower portions of society were catching up. Of course, the bourgeoisie would then do their best to destroy the difference by imitating the new look. And thus fashion as we know it was instituted.

This may or may not be precisely how it happened, but the fact that this has become the story most often told about the emergence of fashion at least alerts us to the fact that its changes are attributed a power that

extends beyond an appeal to the 'trivial' thirst for novelty. Fashion, according to this account, is a system created out of the opposing tug of two forces. The battle
for recognition and acclaim, fought between the upper
and the lower classes, fell into a stalemate around the
issue of dress; whatever move the former made, the latter would always manage to catch up. But this intrac-
table problem eventually took on a life of its own. The
changes began to occur according to a rhythm particular to fashion itself (although this rhythm seeks external justification in its appeal to seasonal changes) and
not according to the whims of anxious royals.

Different from this argument, but nonetheless still
'historical' – or history-esque – is the idea that events
in the world cause people to respond sartorially. This
is the sort of thing you might find in popular histories
of fashion, where clothes are 'explained' in relation to
contemporaneous cultural phenomena. For instance,
in the eighteenth and nineteenth centuries you necessarily cinched in your waist and puffed up your hips
in order to look more nubile because that was the only
way, as a woman, you could be valued. Meanwhile, the
men in your life began to submit to the 'great masculine
renunciation' – the imperative to look really boring in
order to be taken seriously. Then again, in the 1920s,
you naturally lost your feminine curves and donned a
drop-waisted minidress in order to demonstrate your
newfound freedom and political clout. However, in
the 1980s you wisely shunned the miniskirt in favour

The Victorian cinched waist
dress and drop-waisted
dresses in the 1920s

of masculine tailoring as part of your Second Wave
determination to shield your legs from the patriarchy
– although the nicer men around you were getting over
themselves and dabbing on a bit of make-up. In other
words, history tells you what to wear because clothes

and events are in some kind of natural, friendly dialogue. (N.B. No one serious actually thinks this.)

Finally there are those who try to define fashion ahistorically. They may tell us that, on the one hand, there is 'personal style' – a commendable inclination to wear the clothes you actually like and that suit you – as opposed to 'fashion' – a fatuous adherence to a set of arbitrarily imposed commands to wear unflattering, pretentious crap. As Mark-Francis Vandelli, from the British reality show *Made in Chelsea*, has so succinctly stated: 'Fashion is being told what to wear. Style is *knowing*.'

Presumably the truth is woven throughout these four possibilities, and is infinitely more complex than each alone allows. Of course some of those sweaty Sumerians might have preferred to wear diaphanous muslin (not to mention moisture-wicking polyester), but they would have had to wait for the Egyptians to invent it. My 70s dad, for all I know, would have loved to wear a stovepipe hat but most likely couldn't find one in Marks and Spencer. And those upwardly mobile French folk would have been hard pushed to institute the ever-changing fashion system without back-up from the Industrial Revolution. For fashion to come into being, and to cause humans to continue to engage it over the centuries, it must work in numerous ingenious ways.

As with giving up cigarettes, it may be helpful to understand some of the mechanisms at play if we are to have any hope of defending ourselves against the damage done by fashion addiction.

The Infamous Fashion Headfuck

Perhaps it's helpful to begin by unravelling a few of fashion's threads in order to see how it keeps so many of us knotted in. Most visibly, there's competition, desire, production and paranoia – four overlapping forces that flummox us into submission. Like Pringles, whose intensely multi-spiced flavour causes us to keep popping in the hope that we will finally decode what they actually taste of, fashion perhaps overwhelms our critical faculties by simultaneously presenting us with numerous problems, solutions, temptations and failures.

We can set out here by delineating a few of fashion's operative forces, but this can only be in order to show how each one bleeds inextricably into the others in ways that seem guaranteed to make us dizzy.

Competition

Inside this category are further subcategories. There's sexual competition: the right clothes might promise to give us a leg-up by pushing our bodies in the direction of a beauty standard. High heels, corsets, even the less drastic Spanx, may give us hope that we can bag the partner of our dreams, beating off people with naturally longer legs or smaller arses. Then there's status competition – expensive clothes might aim to tell people that we're great at our jobs, talented, or simply independently wealthy, thereby making us more desirable. And finally, and perhaps most twistedly, our impeccable fashion timing – knowing just when to start wearing heavy metal T-shirts, say, then when to stop – may signal that we are impeccably attuned to the zeitgeist and are therefore supremely sensitive and intelligent. We could maybe call this *belle âme* competition, and it's the most overtly fashion-related subcategory, as opposed to simply clothes-related. Of course no one will think you are a beautiful soul if you look at a Gucci advertisement and go straight to the shop and buy the entire outfit. To be a perfect fashion specimen you must get your timing just right, not to mention adding your unique twist to the already-knownness of the current craze.

Desire

Fashion is brilliant at presenting us with things we don't have. One of the logics behind its endless renewals is inversion; sleeves have been wide for a while, so suddenly they must be narrow. Or jeans must stop being skinny and start being baggy. Or go from low-waisted to high-waisted or vice versa. This not only makes it very easy to tell whether someone has the financial means and social savvy to go out and get the correct new stuff, it also makes it easy for designers and producers to generate 'newness', and this 'newness' triggers desire in people who are suddenly revealed – to themselves and others – as not being in possession of the latest thing.

This 'thing' is designated as desirable in as many magazines, shop windows, billboard posters, Instagram posts, etc. as possible, and you just have to take it on trust that if so many people agree that this thing is inherently covetable, then it must be. If you buy it, you will be in possession of the thing everyone seems to want, therefore you're a winner, baby. Suddenly that flouncy dress, stripy top, or drab shade of lipstick – the exact type of thing you professed not to like a month or so before – is catnip to you. You must have it. Of course, once enough people *have* it no one is in a position to *want* it, so if you want to have what other people want you'd better get out there again and shop without delay.

Production

In order for there to be an endless influx of new and desirable objects there has to be the means to make them. Conveniently, as we've fleetingly mentioned, the Industrial Revolution provided an infrastructure of factories, forced labour, exploitation, colonialism and really fantastic machines in order to make sure that the people with the means to do so could get their hands on the objects of their dreams. Naturally, their dreams had to be engineered in such a way as to match the available methods of production, but that turns out not to be so difficult to do. First make the thing, then generate desire for it (using the methods above) and meanwhile get to work in the background on inventing new technology to generate profitable new desires. This logic has gone from strength to strength and it's wonderful to see how tightwad, corner-cutting methods of production can be repackaged and sold back to us as the height of modernist cool. For instance, a type of sewing machine known as a flatlocker made it possible to make stretchy clothes much faster and with less skill. All you had to do was to make contrast top-stitching a desirable design feature and the cash was virtually in the bank. (Stretch fabrics are also good for making your cheap clothes fit as many people as possible.) A few years later, it suddenly became possible to do complex, multicolour embroidery with a machine that made even more economic sense than exploiting a child – just programme the software and a gadget will do the rest – and hey presto the high street was full of darling embroidered blouses.

Perhaps to lend this rather faceless system a little authority, around the mid nineteenth century, in France, there appeared the idea of the genius fashion designer. Whereas before rich people had got together with the finest craftspeople to imagine ornate clothes which were then copied by lesser craftspeople, now there were stroppy, tantrum-throwing artists who told people what to wear. Even rich people. Making fashion a quasi-legitimate art form perhaps had the advantage of legitimising its capricious ways, although it also gave birth to the idea of the 'evil fashion dictator' who tricks stupid people into wearing awful outfits.

The current iteration of this system seems to entail a handful of variously temperamental artistes having their work broken down into easily Google-able words – '80s puff shoulder', 'neon', 'nautical'– and then redesigned by zero-hours fashion graduates who try to incorporate as many search-engine-friendly design features as can be accommodated by a single garment. Puffy shouldered neon sailor top? Google, get me three, in pink, yellow and green!

Paranoia

Paranoia functions as a kind of fashion catalyst, along-side desire. In fashion, the thoughts of others are paramount. Your clothes are basically a form of exter-nalised, visible thinking. Because other people can see your thoughts on this subject so clearly – as soon as you enter any given space – it's a good idea to try to make sure they think well of you. (Or maybe you want them to envy you, or be angry – all good.) Whatever reac-tion you prefer to generate, it will entail having a good understanding of where you sit on British comedian, Eddie Izzard's, 'Circle of Cool'. The Circle takes you on the joined-up journey from 'very cool person' to 'cool adjacent' to 'regular person' to 'looking like a dickhead', which joins back up into 'very cool person' and so on.

In order to locate yourself on the point of the circumference at which you feel most comfortable you need to have a good understanding of both clothes and people. You have to know when and where you can get away with wearing a bondage harness over a dinner shirt and not be seen to scream 'dickhead'. Unfortunately, other people's thoughts and feelings are unpredictable. By trying to find the perfect mid-point between desperate over-egger and normcore slug, you will invariably find yourself pushed off course by the external world which is liable to read you in ways that are at odds with your intentions. You will arrive at new jobs and parties both over- and under-dressed and, to make things worse, might sometimes get things *so* right that certain observers will despise you for it. Basically, fashion repeatedly teaches us that you can't please all people all of the time. There are too many variables to generate even loosely predictable outcomes. Whatever you wear, someone will always hate you for it. Even if that person is just you.

A Wicked Problem

By taking all four possibilities at once perhaps we can begin to glimpse how fashion manages so successfully to torpedo so many of us. It offers us things to want, it exposes us as people who do or don't have access to resources. It makes our thinking around our own self-image painfully visible. It promises to supplement and support us in the social hierarchy, disguising visible 'flaws' and ramping up assets. It makes us feel good about ourselves. And then it makes us feel awful. It's something we both can and can't control. It's the very inconsistency that holds us in thrall. As with other forms of gambling, not knowing in advance whether you will win or lose is precisely what feeds the compulsion. Even if you followed every recommendation in an entire issue of *Dazed and Confused* you would be very likely to come out of it looking and feeling like you'd got something wrong.

And you'd be right. You'd have given away your desperation to be cool, which is congenitally uncool. You'd have done damage to the planet, which is both actually terrible but also, these days, unstylish. You'd have demonstrated lesser fashion credentials than readers of underground Berlin magazines. You'd embarrass those around you who think it's possible, and desirable, to look 'normal'. By trying to be right, right, right, you'd be wrong, wrong, wrong.

Who could invent a system better designed to bewitch a creature so reliant on others, so inclined to imitate, so *social*? In the next chapter we'll look far more closely at the ways in which fashion milks the difficulties of co-existence, promising to alleviate the pain of social injustice and soften the strictures of hierarchies. As we'll see more and more, it's not just underpaid workers on the other side of the world who are being exploited – so are we.

– Status: How Clothes Position Us Socially –

> The question of costume [...] is one of enormous
> importance for those who wish to appear to have what
> they do not have because that is often the best way of
> getting it later on.
>
> – René König

I n the run-up to the twentieth century, at the pro-
tracted and painful birth of modernism, ogling
women in the street became a matter requiring urgent
theorisation. As people scuttled around cities they
clocked each other, and their clothes, and wondered
what on earth to do about it. Other people are so
attractive! But you're probably never going to see them
again! Woe! Men wrote seminal poems and essays
about it, while women kept wearing the clothes.

Baudelaire and Mallarmé can take a great deal
of credit for really tapping into the problem. And
Paris was the place for fleetingly falling in love. But
was it the woman? Or the dress? Or the combination of woman and dress? And what was it about
cities that staged women in dresses so dramatically?
In *The Painter of Modern Life* Baudelaire elides the
seemingly timeless idea of beauty with the idea of

transient fashions, and his poem 'To a Passerby' perfectly encapsulates the romance of alienation: 'Fleeting beauty, By whose glance I was suddenly reborn,
Will I see you no more before eternity?' Meanwhile
Mallarmé's self-published, pseudonymously written
fashion magazine, *La Dernière Mode*, charmingly pres-
ages the least sensible effusions of *Vogue:* 'Whilst the
classic materials of ballgowns aim to envelop us in a
fleeting mist of a hundred shades of white, the dress
itself, on the contrary – both the bodice and the skirt
– is moulded more closely than ever to the body, a
delightful and scientific opposition between the vague
and the (of necessity) definite.'

However, for a really angst-inducing, relatable
essay about clothes and people – and what modern
people might be trying to do with clothes – Georg
Simmel's 'The Philosophy of Fashion' (1901) is hard to
beat. Like Flügel three decades later, Simmel has the
idea that fashion is characterised by an internal contradiction. On the one hand it's about being the same as
other people, but then again it's about distinguishing
yourself. Of course you might argue that this isn't contradictory at all; the point is to be like the admirable
people and unlike the contemptible ones, but it turns
out not to be so simple. If the founding myth of fashion is that it exists because we all want to dress like
the king or queen, Simmel brings out something both
more complex and more elemental. For a start, the
bourgeoisie, by the start of the twentieth century, were

likely to be far more interested in looking like each other than in looking like members of the royal family – especially in France, where there was no longer a royal family to look like. And then there was the fact that fashion was now an industry with its own internal rules and logic which no longer relied on aristocrats. At the heart of this logic was a veritable tug of war. Fashion pitched new against old. It was characterised by creation and destruction. It bound people together and it separated them. It was friendly and hostile, active and passive, organised and chaotic.

Alongside Marx and Nietszche, Darwin was a great influence on Simmel's thinking. We can see in Simmel's theorisation of fashion something of the non-teleological nature of evolution; for both Darwin and Simmel, things evolve, but not necessarily for the better. Simmel is therefore a far better Darwinian than the economist Thorstein Veblen who, in *The Theory of the Leisure Class* (1899), argued that the changing design of clothing was guided by its development in the direction of a more universal pleasingness. Veblen tells us: 'It may be stated broadly that each successive innovation in fashion is an effort to reach some form of display which shall be more acceptable to our sense of form and colour, or of effectiveness, than that which it displaces.' The unfashionable, for Veblen, is something that is left behind by fashion in its onward march toward better days. By contrast, for Simmel, fashion is characterised by senseless mutation; we can't know in advance which mutations will survive and proliferate. One thing we can be sure of, though, is that fashion is anything but a series of improvements – however much it may aim to convince us to ditch our old clothes in favour of new ones. As Simmel suggests: 'We have always to deal with the same fundamental form of duality which is manifested biologically in the contrast between heredity and variation.' Some things stay the same while others change. The changes themselves are unpredictable, but the world then weeds them according to a multitude of forces; some variants prosper while others don't. While nature may not change according to a biannual rhythm of catwalk shows, neither does fashion. Some mutations, like skinny jeans, might last for years whereas others, like moss green knitwear, might stick around for a single season, having barely caught on at all.

Uniql-Oh No You Don't

Of course fashion didn't just arrive fully up and running, and Simmel acknowledges its roots in power relations. A certain group – who might loosely be known as 'the rich' – might want to distinguish themselves visually from other groups. Presumably it's good to know at first glance who's rich and who's poor because then you will quickly know who to marry and who to exploit. People outside your group may envy you and want what you have, in which case they may try to blur the visual distinctions between themselves and you. As we mentioned in the previous chapter, this forces the power group to keep changing its clothes in order to maintain distinctions. However, once you have factories, fashion designers, department stores and magazines, then you have an industrial juggernaut whose momentum isn't simply propelled by the caprices of wealthy individuals. While it might help if a princess wears your stuff once in a while, it's also great if you can get it onto the back of an actress, or even a particularly witty courtesan. In fact, once you have mysterious, metropolitan passers-by you can often just leave it up to them to make the clothes look good. Cities are the perfect spaces for new visual ideas to circulate. If you go for a walk (especially if you are in the aesthetically sensitised state known as convalescence, much romanticised by the early modernists and perhaps also relevant to the Covid era) you will inevitably take in what's hot and what's not. Cities offer endless opportunities for looking and being looked at. As do shared modern spaces, such as trains and stations. Mallarmé noted that train travel necessitated whole new styles of dress. And of course Instagram street-style stars have taken over where the nineteenth-century passer-by left off.

While in the olden days it might have been difficult for the poor, or middle classes, to copy the rich, who tended to keep themselves shut away in exclusive spaces to which they travelled in carriages, in these newly crowded living areas you just had to step out of the front door and open your eyes. Cities also made possible certain breaks with tradition. No longer was it viable to keep tabs on who was who. You could make a fabulous visual impression at the opera and then furtively make your way back to your shabby rented room, leaving everyone to wonder who you were. Of course the old aristocratic system didn't fall apart altogether, it just had to step aside to make way for other social possibilities. Artists, writers and performers developed their own scenes, which might intersect with those of wealthier patrons, but may just as well overlap with outcasts and criminals. Posh boys might be drawn to the exoticism of drug-taking and street fights. There were enough people around that you couldn't possibly know everyone, nor they you, so it was easier to pass yourself off as someone else. This loosening of social positioning opened up greater choices around self-presentation. If you could be anyone, who would you choose to be?

All of which brings us up to today, via two World Wars and the invention of the internet, to a moment where future queens are congratulated for shopping on the High Street and anyone with a smartphone can airbrush themselves to celebrity perfection. Older people can sometimes use medical technology to do quite passable impersonations of younger people, and clothing rental apps now allow you to temporarily dress way beyond your means. On top of this there's no single reliable source of information to help us decide how best to look. In this sense it's not unlike another moment in fashion history. According to Simmel: 'It is said that there was no ruling fashion in male attire in Florence in about the year 1390, because everyone adopted a style of his own.' This was apparently due to the fact that Venetian noblemen had opted to wear low-key black in order to blend in. The reason for such apparent modesty was to obscure the fact that there were so few of them that they might have been easily overpowered. (This may all sound a little unlikely, but at least it's nice to think that our current state of sartorial leaderlessness isn't entirely unprecedented. And that we could gang up to overpower the 1 per cent if only they would stop wearing Uniqlo long enough for us to work out who they were.)

Ever since the demi-mondaines and dandies of nineteenth-century Paris splintered people's ideas of desirable dress, we've seen ever proliferating 'style tribes' (for those old enough to remember this particular eighties obsession) morphing from goths vs

Goths in the 1980s

Sloane Rangers in the last century to cottagecore-hell-princesses (like Kristin Stewart in *Spencer*) in this one. No contemporary style tribe can maintain its purity, nor would it seem to want to. And no matter how idiosyncratically you dress you are at risk of your clothes being swiftly copied and mass produced by fast-fashion companies. If you try to maintain your 'difference', there are the means in place for manufacturers to copy and distribute your personal style worldwide within days. This is precisely what happened to Julia King, a Texan art student, who listed a vintage knitted tank top on Depop in 2020 only to discover a month later that copies of the top could be bought through Amazon, Ali Express, Walmart and Shein. To make things even stranger, her original selfie in the one-off top was being used to sell the mass-produced version around the globe.

Show Me the Money

Is it all just chaos now, or are there still some organising fashion principles? I think you'd have to say that the latter is true, but also perhaps that the former is perfectly designed to obscure it. I guess that's the tricky nature of neoliberalism; it makes it look like anything is possible in order to keep certain systems in place. (The systems that enable the rich to hang onto their money.) So on the one hand you might say that we currently have a much more egalitarian scene where everyone really can wear whatever they like. Gone are the days when you couldn't wear white trainers to exclusive clubs and restaurants – 'white trainers' previously being code for 'the working class and people of colour'. Now white trainers are just as likely to be worn by super-wealthy, white eighty-year-olds (with teeth to match) so can't be used to covertly impose racist and classist agendas. Inversely, if you dress up too much to go out to dinner you might risk being clocked as a cash-strapped interloper who doesn't know that genuine billionaires stick to sportswear while eating. Of course you will still be allowed in, just don't expect too much respect from the waiting staff.

Stealth wealth is perhaps the ultimate contemporary form of snobbish self-presentation. It's sanctimonious and sly, suggesting 'I'm just like you really', while being incredibly difficult to imitate if you're not actually wealthy. Having said that, it often seems to be the case that the super-poor and the super-rich have more in common sartorially these days than the people in the middle. Or at least middle-class kids have the option to horrify their parents by dressing up as Kardashian/Jenners, thereby sending out perplexing messages about where their identifications and aspirations lie; are they aiming upwards or downwards?

Who Wears the Trousers?

It's not just in the field of class relations that fashion

gets up to its mischief. Gender too has been a space of much upheaval. At different periods and in different cultures men and women have clearly had very varied ideas about similarity and distinction between the sexes. If we limit ourselves to modern, industrialised fashion we can see that it gets properly up and running at a time of unusually polarised gender ideals. Whereas the court at Versailles had offered equal opportunities for the wearing of high heels, by the time Marx was railing against the lot of the seamstresses, fashion had largely bifurcated into sensible suits for men and uncomfortable frill-fests for women.

Simmel was writing at a time when it didn't seem unthinkable that women's status might be about to change. Still, it hadn't happened yet, so he acknowledged the possibility of an imminent gender revolution while limiting himself to the idea of femaleness that was largely in circulation at the time. Women were thought to be more bound to convention than men. This he put down to the fact that society offered them very little opportunity or incentive to innovate or dissent. Not only that, they were psychologically unprepared for the kickback one receives when one sticks one's head above the parapet. Women were less educated, but if they nonetheless miraculously managed to do or say something interesting they would be floored by the subsequent attacks. (Maybe no need to point out here that women still take much of the brunt of online hate, and that we often feel unprepared for it.)

Thanks to the restrictions placed on women's agency, fashion became a space in which one could distinguish oneself, or even innovate, without threatening the social order. You might, of course, appear threatening to other less fashionable women, but this suits the system very well. The less women liked each other the easier it was to keep them in order: that way they couldn't gang up on you. Cunningly, this situation also had desirable knock-on effects. If fashion was an arena in which women were allowed to show off, then it also meant that men could show off their women. While it might have been essential for men to demonstrate their seriousness by not partaking in the idiocies of fashionable dress, it was nonetheless great if their wives could wear some ostentatious gear as a demonstration of their husbands' purchasing power. So a woman could both distinguish and denigrate herself while making her husband look big. She could demonstrate superiority to other wives while marking her inferiority to her husband. *And* have her symbolic subordination supplemented by the physical constrictions of cinched waists, crinolines, hobble skirts or uncomfortable shoes.

Thanks to all this, indifference to fashion has tended to be seen as a sign of emancipation, and dress reforms have often been important to political movements, removing distinctions between classes and genders. Simmel tells us that: 'fashion [...] supplements a person's lack of importance'. If that's the only way you can make yourself stand out then . . . well . . . big side eye. However, as with the complexity and distortion around wealth display, so it is with gender. These days, rather than everyone accepting that it's better to wear simple, functional clothes, there is a pull in all directions where men might now feel freer to paint their nails, women might insist they are wearing corsets 'for themselves', and gender-neutral dressing might just as well include pearl earrings as a pair of brogues.

Simmel-taneous Equations

Perhaps more than ever, we have a situation where we are invited to dress intuitively. As it's impossible to follow fashion's ever more twisted and imploding ratiocinations we might as well just do what we like. Still, what we like might very well be informed by what other people seem to like – this appears to be an inevitable aspect of being human.

Perhaps surprisingly, Simmel's essay ends with a swerve towards the spiritual. He tells us: 'When we examine the final and most subtle impulses of the soul, which it is difficult to express in words, we find that they also exhibit this antagonistic play of the fundamental human tendencies. These latter seek to regain their continually lost balance by means of ever new proportions, and they succeed here through the reflection which fashion occasionally throws into the most delicate and tender spiritual processes.' Having argued that fashion somehow dramatises and makes visible the turbulent relations between the haves and the have-nots, simultaneously revealing power imbalances while attempting to ameliorate them, Simmel suddenly comes over all mystical. The 'fundamental human tendencies' he's referring to here are the internal conflicts that tear up our lives. We will always be pulled in different directions – not only by the outside world but by our inner impulses. We want to fit in and stand out, to be accepted for our singularity. The 'most subtle impulses of our souls' are just that – the tiny calibrations that allow us to exist in the world, alongside others, in ways that make sense to us. They tell us what to want and what to reject, how to pitch ourselves in a shared universe.

With fashion, Simmel tells us, we are offered subtle and interesting choices. We might choose to stand out, thereby risking the envy of others. Or to fit in and remain anonymous. Or, perhaps more compellingly than either of those options, we might use the vagaries of fashion to present a front that protects our inner world from the curiosity of others. An interesting enough, contemporary enough veneer might shield us from the incoming gaze, leaving us freer to live out our secret interior lives.

– Fashion as Art –

The faulty assumption here seems to be that the more functionless clothes are, the more like art they become.
– Roberta Smith, *New York Times*, 2013

Arguing against fashion might seem a bit philistine – isn't it a legitimate art form? But then again, isn't it just a scheme for making people continuously buy unnecessary crap? Can it be both? Or is some fashion art – and therefore worth taking seriously – and some just future landfill? How would you know which was which? In order to answer these questions, not only would you have to have a good working definition of fashion, you'd also have to have one of art, and neither is exactly forthcoming.

Perhaps we could agree that fashion is both utterly fatuous and also sometimes sublime. And not necessarily sublime as in overwhelmingly flashy, expensive and beautiful. Yes, there are examples like Alexander McQueen's extraordinary sculptural dresses, but maybe there was also something sublime about the loose-fitting spotty Zara dress that suddenly appeared everywhere, on every type of person, in 2019, as if women had spontaneously agreed to demonstrate a sense of solidarity in opposition to the chauvinist myth of our catty competitiveness. I certainly felt an eruption of excitement every time I saw someone wearing it, as if it somehow signalled a new and better world. Also amazingly, for a mass-produced high street dress, it spared itself from becoming landfill by becoming historic instead. 'THAT ZARA DRESS' can still be bought on eBay for the same price it was originally sold for.

'That' Zara dress

Are You Sitting Comfortably?

Perhaps we could first begin by drawing up a distinction between clothes *in* art and clothes *as* art. In the nineteenth century, as photography was becoming popular, there seems to have been some confusion as to which was more likely to give you a better likeness of a person: a photograph, drawing or painting. Photography had the obvious advantage of being a mechanically rendered document of an actual moment. But this was offset by the fact that – particularly when used to record informal instants – it had an unfortunate habit of making people look quite unlike they imagined themselves to look. In *Seeing Through Clothes* (1978), Anne Hollander's book on dress in art, she describes how women's clothes at that time were structurally complex, built from numerous layers, with a tendency to disregard the wide variety of potential movements of their wearers. When people were photographed doing anything other than standing still as if for a conventional painted portrait they often looked quite ungainly. The intended volumes and lines of their outfits were ruined by whatever they were doing, even if they were just sitting down. There are numerous photographs of women from the middle of the nineteenth century with huge skirts foaming up around their armpits, perched on invisible chairs, the whole piece of furniture having been swallowed by the flounces of their crinolines. Or photographed walking, from behind, with the sashes and ties that held their clothes together in a sad state of disarray. It seemed that, unless photographers behaved like portrait painters, arranging, manipulating and editing their subjects, the resulting pictures wouldn't show what the sitters believed, or hoped, they looked like.

After centuries of people having their portraits painted in their finest rags, photography came along and made a visual muddle. Clothes themselves needed to be rethought in order to get along with this new medium. The first Chanel suits, designed nearly a hun-

The Chanel Suit, 1921

dred years ago, were ideal for being represented photographically. Being relatively flat and fitted to the body, they didn't do anything too weird if you moved around in them. They were the perfect outfit for a world in which your image might be captured unawares.

All of which is to say that the modern era required new ways of dressing. Rather than flamboyantly disregarding the lines of the body, early twentieth-century women's dress (following men's dress, which had cottoned onto this a while back) was more beholden to the underlying shape of the human form. So was the new point in clothes simply to behave themselves in photos?

There were numerous reasons why clothing flattened out in the early twentieth century, including the various waves of dress reform combined with greater equality for women. It no longer seemed so clever to hamper your own movements with decorative clothing that also marked you out as a frivolous person whose thoughts and opinions deserved little attention. There's also the fact that in other fields of design people were busy discovering the beauty of clean lines. In architecture, Art Deco was closely followed by Art Moderne, then functionalism and brutalism. Buildings began to echo the smooth forms of fast-moving objects such as cars and trains, which were designed to flow through space with less resistance. 'Truth to materials' became a catchphrase; it no longer seemed so clever to chisel hard stone into soft curlicues. Art movements such as De Stijl and Cubism mined the aesthetic of simpli-fied forms. Psychoanalysis, too, encouraged people to get real about who they were – to stop trying to whip their own characters and actions into line with restric-tive ideas of moral rectitude. J. C. Flügel's *Psychology of Clothes* (1930) was published at the peak of the modernist project, arguing for the radical honesty of nakedness over the neurotic pretentiousness of dress.

So, was the result of all this to make fashion more boring? And also less 'arty'? If clothes became less flouncy, more streamlined and functional, what room was left for creative expression? But then again, can creativity only express itself through superfluous detail?

When is Now?

The Belgian literary critic Paul de Man, in his article 'Literary History and Literary Modernity' (1971), joins the ranks of people who write fashion off as being a kind of poor cousin to true modernity. (Of course, he's talking about fashions in all things, not just clothes.) He refers to 'the radical impulse that stands behind all genuine modernity when it is not merely a descrip-tive synonym for the contemporaneous or for a passing fashion,' and goes on to say:

Fashion can sometimes be only what remains of modernity after the impulse has subsided, as soon – and this can be al-most at once – as it has changed from being an incandescent point in time into a reproducible cliché, all that remains of an invention that has lost the desire that produced it. Fashion is like the ashes left behind by the uniquely shaped flames of the fire, the trace alone revealing that a fire actually took place.

All of which sounds like a fairly convincing slap in the face for fashion's frequent claims to being innovative and original. The thing that makes fashion 'fashion' is that loads of people copy each other. A new idea is no use in itself – it has to be reproduced. However, you could also argue that fashion, in transforming the 'incandescent point in time into a reproducible cliché', has succeeded in making this dazzling moment into something you can actually perceive and enjoy. The 'new' is perhaps rather like a scream, in that the sound requires the airwaves that carry it as much as the perpetrating voice box; the 'incandescent point' is nothing without the 'reproducible cliché'.

You could say that, in relegating fashion to the status of pale imitator, Paul de Man is guilty of bad faith. He high-handedly denounces fashion in the name of a more elevated moment of innovation, when it's quite clear that *all* instances of creation rely on subsequent repetitions and remodellings in order to achieve their mythical status. Picasso's *Demoiselles d'Avignon*, for example, might have seemed to some to be a stand-alone masterpiece but – apart from the fact that early modernist movements such as impressionism made it possible – it's also the fact that it exerted an influence on so many subsequent artworks that makes it a modernist marvel. Without this follow-up it would be just a lonely, wonky painting.

To come back to the question of fashion, art and functionality, it's not hard to see why Roberta Smith, the *New York Times*' chief art critic, might have a go at fashion writers and curators who seem to suggest that functionality and art are in some kind of antithetical relationship. Or at least that you can rely on the fact that your clothes are impossible to wear to elevate them to fine art status. For example, Hussein Chalayan's famous coffee-table skirt – literally a hard, wooden skirt that doubles as a table – can't guarantee

Hussein Chalayan's coffee-table skirt, 2000

its own art status just by being completely unsuited to being worn in daily life. It also has to pose questions about women, domesticity and value. Or maybe to make people ask themselves what on earth is the purpose of a catwalk show. And even then not everyone would agree that it's the radical masterpiece some fashion people like to portray it as. Some might say it's not particularly innovative as fine art and not remotely influential as fashion – it certainly made no mark whatsoever on the way people dress.

Alternatively, an ensemble like Vetements' pink ombre tracksuit from their S/S23 collection seems genuinely challenging in terms of ideas like 'good taste', 'high value' and 'dressing up'. An outsize, floppy tracksuit emblazoned with the slogan I'M NOT DOING SHIT TODAY, the outfit references hopelessly unstylish, purely-for-comfort pandemic dressing – something other fashion houses, like art tryhards Prada, seem desperate to rush us out of. The look could be described as post-postmodern; it has elements of the readymade but amplified and distorted into a colour-saturated, Insta-friendly, de-realised sculptural oddity. It's confrontational, unnerving and undeniably beautiful, and seems certain to make an impact on real people's clothing at the same time as opening up questions about femininity, wealth, productivity, elegance, desirability and any number of troublesome ideas around self-presentation. In short, it's a polysemantic masterpiece.

Pink ombre tracksuit by Vetements

Why would we have the idea that fashion and art are in any sort of relationship anyhow? Apparently the question can be directly referred back to the dress designer, Charles Frederick Worth, who became famous as the court designer for Napoleon III in the mid 1800s. As Elizabeth Wilson explains in her book, *Adorned in Dreams* (1985): 'It was only from this time that fashionable womenswear was seen as the creation of a single designer – just at the time when a clothing industry and mass-produced fashion were beginning to appear. Consequently the exclusive dress has to be definitively distinguished from the vulgar copy; the dress designer had to become an Artist.' Worth apparently took the idea quite literally, dressing up as Rembrandt in the floppy beret and smock that have since become the clichéd garb of the deep and sensitive artiste.

The designer-as-artist was a concept that brought numerous advantages. It was great for the women who wore the clothes as the garments brought instant cachet, and it was wonderful for the designers as their cultural promotion encouraged them to be whimsical, 'inspired' people who could therefore not only charge loads of money, but could also behave like raving despots. This must have been a total pain for the people close to them, but is enduringly enjoyed at a distance if the success of the Netflix series *Halston* (staring Ewan McGregor as the American fashion designer and autocratic monster) is anything to go by. Or Paul Thomas's *Phantom Thread.* People can't help loving a cranky, self-absorbed artist, apparently.

Suit Yourself

Gilles Lipovetsky, in his book, *The Empire of Fashion* (1987), has quite a different take on the whole question of art, fashion and industrial design. For a start, he argues that recent sociological developments suggest we ought seriously to question the ongoing relevance of Herbert Spencer's class distinction story as the founding myth of fashion. Lipovetsky aims to demonstrate that fashion is less about competition and more about marking out your own individuality, and claims that modern consumerism is driven by the shopper's desire to please him- or herself rather than by a rivalrous desire to impress others (although he doesn't deny that this second impulse has its place). What needs to change in our attitude to fashion, apparently, is not our misplaced obedience, as Veblen and Flügel might tell us, but our paradigm for understanding what motivates us to wear it. According to Lipovetsky, fashion logic has consumed all areas of life. Western production values are uniformly based on the values that proved so successful for haute couture – the system that originated when Charles Frédéric Worth opened his 'fashion house' in the Rue de la Paix in winter 1857–8. As a production ethos, haute couture can be characterised by its composite motivations of profit and sovereign artistic invention. Haute couture garments were intended to sell, but their main selling point was their innovativeness. Lipovetsky tells us:

When newness asserts itself as the supreme requirement, a second requirement necessarily accompanies it in the short or the long run: the couturier's independence becomes legitimate and obligatory. Hence the existence of a separate agency entirely devoted to creative innovation, detached from the ineluctable conservatism and inertia of social demand. The headlong advance of modern fashion [. . .] was possible only thanks to the modern ideal of newness and its corollary, creative freedom.

Although haute couture remained very expensive, and therefore only available to a small number of people, the fact that it was made according to the whims of a sovereign creator, who in turn produced vast numbers of 'models' for sale to exclusive buyers, made it a mode of production in close harmony with the 'ideological referents of democratic individualism'. Fashion designers became stars in their own rights, while the women who wore fashion maintained an appearance of uniqueness thanks to the proliferation of novel and surprising designs.

Throughout this time, right up until the 1950s, the only access less-than-wealthy people had to the concoctions of haute couture were poorer quality mass-produced imitations. During the post-war economic boom, designers in America and France – led by Yves St Laurent – decided to cash in on the widespread fascination with fashion, and began to produce their own ready-to-wear collections. These were far cheaper than their haute couture counterparts but, unlike previous mass-manufactured garments, weren't necessarily degraded copies of more prestigious originals: ready-to-wear clothes could be fashionable on their own terms.

This mode of production, whereby high-quality products aim right from the start to be accessible to as many people as possible (rather than having to pass through several stages of degeneration before finally conquering the 'bottom' end of the market) is, according to Lipovetsky, what informs all areas of contemporary manufacture. By the close of the twentieth century, kitchen appliances, stereos, cars, etc, were thus developed in accordance with fashion logic in two respects. Firstly, they had to be continuously re-invented, and these innovations must, thanks to their sheer quantity, make room for individual preferences – a sound system must come with innumerable optional functions, allowing the purchaser to find the item that perfectly suits them (in the manner of haute couture). And secondly, in order to stay in business, the 'quality' or 'name' brands must produce articles at a price that makes them available at all levels of the social strata (in the mode of ready-to-wear).

In opposition to the plethora of post-Marxist theorists who tell us that modern consumerist society aims to alienate people from things, each other and themselves, Lipovetsky insists that people buy new appliances – with familiar logos – because the products are actually useful and/or gratifying. In a burst of idealism seemingly informed by 1980s happy-clappy consumerism, he insists that 'we are living in an era in which use value is getting its revenge over status value: private enjoyment is winning out over honorific value.' Due to the restructuring of the market in such a way as to dispense with the need for aristocratic role-models, consumers are free to choose the things they actually like, rather than the things they think other people will like them for.

From here, Lipovetsky develops the idea of the 'fashion person'; someone whose tastes endlessly fluctuate in synch with the latest crazes. Unlike the tragic character dominated in public and private by the demands of a diabolical society (as envisioned by left-wing social theorists), Lipovetsky's fashion person welcomes the continuously expanding sets of possibilities opening up before him. The system of consummate fashion creates receptive mentalities characterised by fluidity that are inherently prepared for the adventure of the new.

Lipovetsky is not so naïve as to think that the advent of this delightful figure is enough to make the world a perfect place. The fashion person has been born into a world of 'economic spirals, the escalation in war technology, terrorist attacks, nuclear catastrophes, unemployment, the distribution of labour, xenophobia' and so on. And, while he is far from oblivious to all of this, the only hope of motivating him into doing something to change it is to offer him a highly personal incentive, or to make sure that any incitement to activism also involves the promise of a showbiz party.

In spite of his hedonism, however, the 'fashion person' is still capable of unhappiness. But, unlike the cruelly oppressed figure described by the post-Marxists, he imagines that it is within his power to cheer himself up. For Lipovestky (and pretty much all other social theorists, as we are beginning to see) fashion is double-edged. On the bright side, it enables you to 'be yourself' (whatever that means). But on the downside, it makes you doubt that self – is that really the best self you can come up with? – at the same time as cutting you loose from the social contract.

If this is where an adherence to the myth of the great artist lands us, perhaps we need to look at other ways of thinking about art. In the 90s many artists began to move away from the production of one-off objects for sale to oligarchs and arms dealers (and that's if their careers were going *well*) and began to think instead in terms of 'encounters'. What was exciting about everything from the *Mona Lisa* to Jeff Koons' *Puppy* was the fact that you could 'meet' it in real life. But couldn't other kinds of 'meeting' also be exciting? Rikrit Tiravanija made entire exhibitions that existed solely of serving food to visitors to the gallery, and the 'art shop' became a popular form in itself. From Tracy Emin and Sarah Lucas's seminal 90s East End emporium, to Christine Hill's Berlin *Volksboutique* and *The Sarah Staton Supastore*, shops were used by artists as spaces in which to explore what it means to buy and sell, see and be seen, speak and be spoken to. These weren't just spaces where artists flogged their work – the entire shop *was* art; a walk-in installation, inviting you to think about the nature of display and exchange. If the white cube commercial gallery space became faux sacred – to the point where sales and money had to be handled in back rooms, keeping the exhibition areas 'pure' – the art shop was more frank about the nature of transactions; they were foregrounded, fun, notable, a thing in themselves. And, more than that, they weren't necessarily monetary. At Hill's *Volksboutique* (literally 'people's shop') visitors could stop by to swap clothes, drink tea and have a chat.

Since the 90s, art has perhaps moved further and further away from the hegemony of the 'big man' and more towards collectives, socially engaged art practices, and the subversion of traditions like prizes for individuals; in 2020 it became increasingly difficult to give a prize to a lone person – it had become a point of principle for many artists to pool resources and to refuse to compete. This seems a much better model for thinking about the future of fashion. People can still make and wear amazing things, but in a hyper-social, inclusive way.

– Horror: The Body in Fashion –

There's blood beneath every layer of skin.
– Alexander McQueen

K oumpounophobia – a fear of buttons – is a surprisingly common psychological symptom. In psychoanalytic work one comes across it from time to time. It tends to be quite mystifying to the sufferer; it's rare for anyone to report a directly button-related trauma. It's also unusual for it to be the main presenting problem. The person may not mention it except as an afterthought. After free-associating around it loosely now and again the person may notice that buttons are hard objects that penetrate through soft openings. They also control access to the naked body – in the case of a man's shirt they are often the last layer of defense. Buttons become frightening because of their association with nakedness and sexuality – the very things they are designed to cover up.

As Flügel so persuasively explained, clothes are paradoxical; they hide the body and draw attention to it. Sometimes they do this quietly, as is the case with an understated suit. Sometimes they make a play of doing it noisily, like Kate Moss in a transparent red dress with a leopard print leotard underneath. In Ana Lily Amirpour's *A Girl Walks Home Alone at Night* the main character's costume is literally and semantically layered. 'The Girl' wears a Jean Seberg style striped Breton top underneath her black chador – a garment that's perhaps famous for its hyperbolic approach to obscuring the female form. Not only do her black robes echo those of Count Dracula, but she glides along on a skateboard, with the suggestion that, like a supernatural figure, she may not have a body at all. Clothes form a complex relationship with the body at the best of times, but in horror movies things go from bad to worse. Here, the body itself – or at least the skin – isn't the last layer. It's liable to be broken open, its limits totally disrespected. The 'wholeness' of a body is repeatedly shown to be a thing you only get to hang onto if you're lucky.

Anyone who went to art school in the nineties was forced to read Jacques Lacan's seminal 1949 essay 'The Mirror Stage as Formative of the Function of the *I* as Revealed in Psychoanalytic Experience'. It's a brilliant explanation of why human beings feel crappy and inauthentic so much of the time.

To oversimplify wildly, you have a human infant who's uncomfortable in its own skin, which is why it cries so much. Babies don't know what's them, what's not them, or what the hell is going on. Then, at around the age of six months – once their nascent cognitive faculties are sufficiently up and running – they are suddenly able to grasp the notion that the thing they see reflected back in a mirror is *them*. Not only that, but these creatures that circle around them – their family or whoever – are separate from them. Even more amazingly, they themselves are one of these beings. This is an incredibly exciting revelation for a baby, who inevitably experiences itself as rather fragmented and desperate – it can't control anything much, certainly not its own body, and just has to scream and hope for the best. But then it catches a glimpse of itself as a cohesive entity and gets its hopes up. The image it sees in the mirror appears more advanced and more perfect than the messy reality it inhabits; the reflection is a promise of future mastery. There's a moment of absolute jubilation . . . followed by a lifetime of disappointment caused by trying to live up to the promise of that moment – as if the mirror was saying: 'One day you too will be one of those autonomous creatures that does interesting stuff while you just squirm around.' And while it might be the case that most people do indeed grow up and learn to walk and talk and use cutlery, it's also bound to be true that your more trained and socialised body will continue to be haunted by traces of its chaotic, helpless origins.

You might say that babies are like people who put up heavily perfected photos on Instagram, feel really pleased with themselves, and then have to deal with the sad fact that it's just a filtered photo while simultaneously being fated to get on with being their divided, contradictory, acne-scarred selves. That's the tragedy of the human condition according to Lacan; constant alienation. The mirror image helps us to understand something about what we are, but it also condemns us to constantly fall short of our own expectations; it presents us with a better, easier version of ourselves, but it's an image rather than an embodied experience.

Fashion is absolutely brilliant at either exploiting and/or helping out with this situation, depending on how you look at it. On the one hand you have the idea that the fashion industry makes everyone feel bad about themselves – and you hear enough from models to fully support this point of view – but then again you have the side of fashion that actually helps us to enjoy inhabiting our bodies. It gives us different shapes and colours to experiment with and offers a general defamiliarising effect which can be an incredible relief, even if it's only temporary. The system of constant, regular change means that there's always a new thing out there to identify with – an image that invites us to inhabit it. We see this newly introduced style of clothing, and a person looking really good in it – really complete, possibly a bit self-satisfied, apparently getting lots of narcissistic enjoyment – and think: 'Wow, if I wore something like that I too might feel more complete and happy in myself.' It sounds idiotic, but of course it's not, it's just a re-dramatisation of the fundamentally structuring infantile moment of excitement and recognition. You can put new clothes on and, while they're still strongly linked with an external image, you can enjoy the satisfying alienation. You're temporarily Other to yourself. Not for long, but just long enough to get a bit of relief. It's a little Cinderella-like – especially when the magic wears off and you realise it's crappy old you again. But that's OK because by then it should be time for a new set of identifications.

Lacan himself didn't discuss fashion much at all, although he was obviously obsessed with it, spending loads of money on impeccable tailoring, weird Austin Powers blouses and horrible fur coats. There is, however, one very striking mention of fashion, in his essay 'Aggressivity in Psychoanalysis' from 1948. Strangely enough for a text that deals with the split between wholeness and fragmentation, the essay itself is also considered the darker counterpart to the sunnier mirror phase text. If the 1949 paper foregrounds the lovely (if tormenting) mirror image, this other essay focusses on the mess that the image attempts to ameliorate. In it, Lacan mentions the bodily mutations so graphically depicted by Hieronymous Bosch, and alludes to the 'septet of baby fears' drawn up by the post-Freudians (or, to be more precise, that raving homophobe, Edmund Bergler): 'images of castration, emasculation, mutilation, dismemberment, dislocation, evisceration, devouring and bursting open of the body'. In this context Lacan goes on to talk about some of the things people voluntarily put their bodies through – tattooing, incision and circumcision – before pointing to what he calls 'the procrustean arbitrariness of fashion'.

According to Greek mythology, Procrustes was a bandit who kept a house by the side of a road often used by travellers. He would offer passers-by a place to sleep for the night, claiming he had a special bed that perfectly fitted any size of person. What he failed to mention was that he would strap the visitor to the bed and either stretch or amputate them in order to get the fit just right. So here, Lacan is putting fashion in the series of social practices that 'contradict [. . .] the natural forms of the human body'. By pulling in waists, revealing shoulders, hiding necks, lengthening legs, padding out bottoms, or compacting them, fashion works against our bodies as much as it works with them. We might think we use clothes to support our illusion of bodily unity, but actually our clothes may be conspiring against us, stealthily cutting us up.

Costume Drama

In horror movies, as a rule, bad things happen to bodies. They get burned, boiled, branded, slashed, crushed and torn. Very often these things happen to the most beautiful and pristine of bodies. Sometimes these bodies are dressed in the finest clothes. In Guillermo del Toro's *Crimson Peak* (2015) the ornate Victorian dresses are so staggeringly lovely that one worries for their safety. Still, they also look good a bit shredded, covered in mud and blood. While *Crimson Peak* wasn't a great success at the box office it is already spoken about as a cult movie. Anyone who's seen it seems to agree that it isn't particularly scary. Nor is it a very original story; quite the opposite, it's a generic gothic romance. The main thing about it is the way it looks – the cinematography and clothes, which are impeccably inhabited by the actors. Some might want to argue that this isn't enough to carry a whole movie, but that's perhaps because they don't know how to look. The thing about the clothes in *Crimson Peak* is that they are characters and they *act*. They don't just hang about on the actors' bodies waiting for something to happen. They respond to events themselves. This might not be clear the first time you see it – I certainly didn't notice it consciously – but the overall effect is weirdly warm and enveloping. Watching the film is something like being swaddled. And what is swaddling if not a demonstration of the soothing-yet-frightening power of fabric?

In interviews about the movie the costume designer, Kate Hawley, spoke about the multiple copies of dresses – and especially nighties – that had to be made for each scene. Not only did they have to be slashed and splashed, then spring back to their original perfection for a re-take, they also had to express emotion. At times they would be puffed up with undergarments, at others they were allowed to be floppy. Sleeves, apparently, were one of the biggest variables. Del Toro wanted them as big as possible, but sometimes they had to shrink right down to accentuate the smallness and fragility of the character. The furniture too would expand and contract to make the baddies appear bigger and the goodies smaller. At the beginning of the film, when the heroine Edith Cushing (played by Mia Wasikowska, who began her career as a model) is robust and healthy, she dresses in glowing gold, her sleeves billowing extravagantly. But when she finds herself being gradually poisoned, she flops down in a gigantic armchair, her frail arms in tight, white bandage-like sleeves. Her evil sister-in-law (Jessica Chastain) is often dressed in cold-blooded blue. Chastain apparently wore seven-inch plastic stripper shoes concealed under her ornate late nineteenth-century dresses to give her a towering appearance. These, combined with tight corsets and heavy wigs, gave her such headaches, and made her so uncomfortable, that some of her acting was underpinned by genuine pain; her costumes were literally attacking her. While the film's title refers to the characters' quasi-alive family pile, perhaps it's the clothes that are really haunting. Unlike the house, you never actually see the garments get up to their mischief. They're not so hammy as to make their uncanny purposes known.

Another film that's striking for its treatment of beauty, fashion and horror is Veronika Franz and Severin Fiala's *Goodnight Mommy* (2014). Unusually, the first bodily mutilation happens before the film begins; the main character has had a facelift. She is convalescing in her secluded minimalist pad with only her ten-year-old twin sons for company. The boys are spooked by their mother's heavily bandaged face, refusing to believe that this cold, quiet woman is really her. If she'd hoped to make herself appear more perfect, her surgery has only opened up questions for her children about what kind of creature they are really dealing with. The surface appearance of the film is impeccably tasteful, from the minimalist furnishings to the mother's expensive-looking, neutral house clothes. But this attempt at perfection is doomed, ultimately only succeeding in revealing the horror that lies a skin's depth away.

While *Crimson Peak* is charmingly old-fashioned, harking back to the days of fainting hysterics in preposterously impractical clothes, *Goodnight Mommy* has a more contemporary take on the limits of the body. Here, flesh and blood are treated almost like another dress – something that can easily be adjusted if it stops fitting. But it turns out not to be so simple, and this very pragmatism is what causes everything to fall apart.

If *Crimson Peak* is among the most comforting of horror films, *Goodnight Mommy* is one of the least. In the former film everything is alive; clothes, chairs, mud. Bad things happen to bodies, but even then they come back. Mothers and wives never *really* die. Their ghosts might look a bit nasty but they're generally trying to save you from something. The world it depicts is extravagantly, magnificently empathic and responsive;

it's the ultimate wish-fulfilling fantasy. By contrast, the world as shown in *Goodnight Mommy*, in keeping with its modernist aesthetic, is ruled by the laws of physics. The ghosts aren't really ghosts, the dead are truly dead, and the living are liable to treat their own bodies like 'stuff' that can be spliced and edited. However, what both films share is the idea that our clothes are anything but extraneous and passive.

– Harm: How Our Clothes Can Hurt Us –

Perhaps enough has been said elsewhere about the many ways in which fashion harms the environment, not to mention the people who make the actual clothes. Fashion was much written about by both Marx and Engels, who seemed to be in agreement that luxury garments are the perfect exemplar of the beauty and horror of capitalism. You could almost say that *Capital Volume I* is a book about clothes. Way before people in developing countries were stitching SOS messages into Primark garments, Marx was devoting hundreds of pages to the deadly maltreatment of seamstresses. In fact, he actually uses the word 'murderous' to describe their working conditions. At the same time he acknowledges that under capitalism people come up with really brilliant stuff – which is necessary otherwise we'd all opt out of it immediately.

Here, perhaps it's more useful to try to speak about a different form of harm; self-harm by means of fashion. It often seems to appear alongside other forms of self-harm, like cutting, extreme dieting, drugs, anorexia, financial self-harm or even getting into physical fights. Unlike many other forms of self-harm it usually doesn't need to be kept hidden, and can instead be put on full display, although people might sometimes have quite a furtive attitude towards the acquisition of garments, perhaps hiding from partners how much they spend or how many things they buy. One of the first instances I saw of it, clinically, was with a woman who went on a massive spending spree in the week before she made a serious suicide attempt. After coming out of hospital, she returned some of the clothes, but kept a cashmere coat as a kind of expensive memento. She saw the two activities – shopping and taking an overdose – as being closely linked, as if the shopping had been a milder form of self-harm; an attempt to stave off the later, more damaging one. It's also probably important to mention that she had used her husband's credit card, perfectly demonstrating the way in which self-harm is often bound up with violence directed at others.

I've never heard of anyone coming to therapy explicitly asking to be cured of their interest in fashion. If people speak about it at all in sessions it's usually once they've been coming for a while, and they may even say they feel awkward talking about something so trivial. In that sense you could say that people experience more awkwardness talking about fashion than about sex, at least when they're on the couch.

Let's return briefly to Lacan's aggressiveness essay, which deals with the 'corps morcelé', or fragmented body, and the ways in which this haunts us. The peculiar word use in the title – which is translated as 'aggressivity' or 'aggressiveness' rather than the more usual 'aggression' – is perhaps to differentiate it from actual instances of anger or violence. The word aims at an aggressiveness that seeps into everything, or lays in wait constantly to disrupt any idealised image. If the too-perfect specular image is persecutory, it's in part due to the fact that it acts as a reminder of the thing it aims to disavow; the uncomfortable chaos of life in a body. The essay ranges over all sorts of different phenomena, from the way analysands might express aggressiveness through small actions, obvious falsifications, missed sessions, and so on, to the depictions of bodily disarray you find in horror movies. Images of horror are held up as being as important, and fundamental, as the 'organising' image of the complete, discrete body. If you have the latter, you're always going to have the former. Order and chaos go hand in hand.

There are certain people who seem to have a particular talent for incarnating both sides of the equation. The Australian performance artist Leigh Bowery, who died in 1994, would use padding to create extreme bodily asymmetry, cover himself in a graphic rash, squash his face under sheer tights or strap a fully-grown woman under his crimplene dress and give birth to her half an hour or so into a performance with his band, Minty. Similarly, Anna Piaggi, the eighties Italian fashion writer, was known for her extreme outfits. One year she apparently travelled between the Paris, Milan and London shows by train because her crinolines couldn't be accommodated by aeroplane seats – and she couldn't bring herself to wear anything else for the flight. Isabella Blow, the British stylist and magazine editor, was a great ambassador for the designs of Alexander McQueen and the milliner Phillip Treacy, once wearing a beautiful hat made from an explosion of multiple pairs of lips that obscured most of her face. And Violet Chachki, along with so many other amazing drag queens, shows an extraordinary capacity to walk in impossible heels, while tucked and cinched to the point of being seemingly about to snap in half – and all of it while cracking jokes or dancing.

Violet Chachki

Lacan seems to be in agreement with other psychoanalytic commentators on fashion, focussing on its disregard for comfort or practicality, and its tendency to treat the body with a certain carelessness or even cruelty. It's interesting that he mentions Bosch, as contemporary fashion designers also seem to be quite interested in the Dutch painter and there are numerous instances of his paintings appearing on clothes. *The Garden of Earthly Delights* has been directly referenced at Alexander McQueen, Valentino, Dior, Carven, Undercover and Gucci. But then again some of these designers (perhaps especially Jun Takahashi at Undercover and Alessandro Michele at Gucci) have a geeky, theoretical approach to clothes, so quite possibly read Lacan for inspiration.

As we are seeing, in psychoanalytic literature – and elsewhere – fashion appears again and again as ambiguous, both good and evil, something that shares with the psychoanalytic symptom a structure of enjoyment and suffering, pleasure and pain, irritation and relief. On the one hand clothes can supposedly help you out with embodied life, conceal the bits you feel ashamed of and accentuate the bits you're proud of. But then again, there's this system called fashion that isn't really about clothes in any practical sense, but about the endless replacement of clothes by other clothes. And especially the vilification of certain clothes and extreme elevation of others. As we have said, it's a system that's perfect for producing the kind of anxiety that keeps people captivated. As Lacan notes else-where in his essay on aggressiveness, psychoanalysis induces a 'controlled paranoia' (i.e. you try to work out what your psychoanalyst thinks of you, but you can't) which can be a motor for clinical work. In an unlikely echo, perhaps fashion could be said to do the same. If it's a game around trying to control who you are for the Other (which, for Lacan, would be a way of trying to ameliorate anxiety) it's also a game where the rules can change suddenly and capriciously so you can never fully be sure where you stand.

Perhaps this explains in part the appeal of the con-cept of the 'evil fashion person' so often repeated in contemporary portrayals of the business. Fashion can make us feel terrible, but it can be hard to say quite why. Enter the fashion meanie; someone who knows exactly how to make us suffer. In *The Devil Wears Prada*, *Zoolander* and *Cruella*, we see various por-trayals of the archetypal fashion villain – sociopathic characters who only care about their own prestige and self-advancement and don't give a hoot about the pain of others. For a real-world account of the nasti-ness of fashion, in the documentary *McQueen*, Alexan-der McQueen speaks about suddenly finding himself working at the 'evilest' end of the fashion industry. By this he doesn't mean the most exploitative or environ-mentally destructive, but the most personally unpleas-ant. In trying to explain something about his spiral into addiction and extreme unhappiness he alludes to something malignant operating in his field. In another example from life, in 2017 the Freud Museum hosted a conversation between the clothes designer, Bella Freud, and fashion writer and muse, Amanda Harlech. Given free rein to speak unguardedly about their experiences of working in fashion, the entire conversation revolved around the outlandish spite of many of their colleagues. Harlech, in particular, reported numerous instances of backhanded compliments and negging by fashion PRs and assistants, mainly centering on her physical appearance and unfortunate choice of clothes. At the time I thought they were exaggerating, or even trying to imply that their well-rewarded, high-status jobs weren't that enviable after all (i.e. they were patronising their lowly, civilian audience) but a few days later I was invited to do a webcast with a well-known influencer who introduced herself by saying that she'd tried to find out a bit about me but there wasn't a single shred of evidence of my existence anywhere online. I hope she's better at influencing people than she is at making friends. In short, it seems possible that there are certain people who are very adept at using the paranoia inherent in the fashion system to destabilise others in a wild attempt to bolster their own egos.

So it's basically agreed across the board, from political theorists to psychoanalysts to intelligent designers like McQueen, that it's an extremely problematic terrain. On the one hand it has incredible allure and seems to promise people a lot in terms of desirability and social status, but at the same time it impoverishes, disappoints and frustrates us. It makes sure we can never be fully satisfied with what we have, that there will always be something else. Fashion can make us physically uncomfortable, socially uncomfortable, not to mention occasionally killing the people who make it, while also destroying the environment. No amount of decolonising *Vogue* can undo all that.

If you speak to people over time in psychoanalysis it often becomes apparent that their relationship with the things they wear isn't easy. Either they feel that everyone else is better dressed than them, or they overspend, or get into relentless cycles of ordering and returning, or wear their mother's designer hand-me-downs and feel annoyed and resentful. In my analytic work I see all sorts of things, from the suicidal woman to a woman who would fantasise about self-harm but never act on her fantasies, instead spending every spare minute of her time doing things to her clothes, cutting them, reshaping them, adding bits of one thing to another thing. She had a totally Frankensteinish approach to clothing even the vocabulary around it seemed significant: cutting, slashing, dyeing, not to mention the occasional vicious purge.

My own first analyst – a Kleinian – tried to cure me of my fascination with fashion in my mid twenties and I found the idea infuriating. It wasn't a symptom I had any interest in dropping; I had certainly never asked him to help me with it. He was totally right to pick up on it though. Every week on the way to see him I would visit a second-hand clothes shop – appropriately named 'Hang-Ups' – and spend my student grant on clothes I didn't need. I would talk about how I would like to travel and make well-produced video art, but that my constant pennilessness got in the way. I would be sitting there telling him this while dressed in head-to-toe discarded John Galliano, with that week's haul in a large paper bag at my feet. He would say: 'Maybe you could try buying fewer clothes,' to which I would reply: 'But they were so cheap for what they are, it would have been irresponsible not to grab them'. Although I knew his point was backed up by irrefutable logic, the impulse to keep shopping was so strong that he never managed to make a dent in it. (And now I have a rack of priceless early Galliano pieces so maybe I'm giving the guy too much credit.)

Fashion and Waste

In Marie Kondo's TV series, clothes go first. In house after house we see these soft piles of disappointment, their owners seemingly filled with disgust at the sight of them. How did they come to own so many useless garments? Were they asleep while they were buying them? One counter-intuitive, unconscious temptation fashion may hold for us is revealed in the fact that the production of waste is literally central to its workings. The French writer, George Bataille, points this out in

Visions of Excess (1927–1939), where he talks about the 'complex conditions' created specifically for the purposes of generating losses in public sports such as horse racing. He says: 'The ostentatious display of the latest luxury fashions' is an important adjunct to the 'unproductive expenditure' of great competitive spectacles. Like spending large amounts of money on any ephemeral display – such as fireworks – buying clothes whose primary value lies in the fact that they will soon have to be replaced and discarded gives us some experience of the thrill of squandering.

Any fashion item, from the moment it appears, openly betrays a trace of its future unfashionableness. The freshest, most desirable garment has its fate written all over it. But what if the relentless disappearances of fashion were an attempt at a controlled experiment with loss? Through new clothes, we are offered the promise of an immaculate, unbroken body which we invest in and inhabit until its novelty wanes and our bodies begin to refragilise. These 'failed' clothes are cast out and new ones brought in to fulfil the old one's promises. So the continuous losing of the unified body is tempered by the continuous possibility of gaining it. But the potentially endless disappointment of this scheme (which, unrectified, might result in its own downfall) is perhaps turned around by the secret pleasure with which the disastrous ex-fashion is discarded. What if waste was a delicious revenge against clothing for its failure to make us feel good about ourselves?

Whereas the fashion system may at first seem to be attempting to control loss by always having something new with which to replace the discarded object, loss may in fact be controlling the system. Instead of being a by-product, the debris of fashion may be one of the driving forces behind it. You could argue that fashion is a very elaborate reprisal against the ego's inhibiting attempts at constraining the body. Returning to Herbert Spencer's founding myth of fashion we could perhaps say that the restrictive ego is represented by the aristocracy, which tries to control the seething masses' clothes in order to diminish the threat of its ascendancy. By this account fashion is an evasive measure on behalf of the multitude (the riotous body) against the limiting regulations inflicted on it.

– Beauty and Ugliness:
Fashion as Unlikely Redeemer –

> Gratitude is liberating. It builds a sense of sufficiency
> that is quite subversive to the consumer society.
> – Joanna Macy, *World as Lover, World as Self*

The idea of the 'emperor's new clothes' is so often used in analogies – about art, science, terrorism, even workplace harassment – it's easy to forget that it's actually a story about . . . *clothes.* For Thorstein Veblen, the main obstacle to modern Western fashion reaching an ideal and therefore stable form was its obedience to the law of expensiveness, which decreed that clothes need not be designed to be beautiful, but merely to look obviously new – and thus clearly recently purchased. This insistence on newness, he believed, was the very thing that made the garments ugly. You couldn't keep churning out endless innovations and have them all look great; some, if not most, were necessarily going to be clangers. In opposition to this we have Baudelaire's idea of the incandescent charm of the new. For Baudelaire, the novelties of fashion are inherently beautiful; they're a visible manifestation of the exciting evanescence of life lived in real time – nature unadorned is what's ugly.

It's rare to hear an account of Hans Christian Anderson's fairy tale that suggests the emperor might have looked gorgeous with his kit off. One exception is Robert Altman's 1994 film *Prêt-à-Porter*, which ends with a naked catwalk show, and the suggestion that we're somehow better off without the inhibiting artifices of fashion. (He may very well have read Flügel. Lots of people do. A nameplate in my second-hand copy tells me it used to belong to Desmond Morris, author of *The Naked Ape*.) Having said that, it's very few people's favourite film – let alone their favourite Altman film – so perhaps this can tell us something about how convincing people find that idea.

This divergence of opinion sets up another of fashion's oppositions. On the one hand it's all about wealth, exclusivity and rarified beauty. On the other it makes people look ugly, strange and stupid. For those less in thrall to binaries, you might say the two possibilities are somehow fused, and that this is another part of what gives fashion its Pringle-like, sublime flavour. Judging by Diana Vreeland's account of a Balenciaga show, the impact of seeing new clothes can be quite intense. In her autobigraphy, *D.V,* she tells us: 'One never knew what one was going to see at a Balenciaga opening. One fainted. It was possible to blow up and die. I remember one show in the early sixties [. . .] Audrey Hepburn turned to me and asked why I wasn't frothing at the mouth at what I was seeing. I told her I was trying to act calm and detached because, after all, I was a member of the press. Across the way, Gloria Guinness was sliding out of her chair onto the floor. Everyone was going up in foam and thunder. We didn't know what we were doing, it was so glorious.' When encountering fashion, it seems, it can be hard to know what's hit you. Is it good, bad, nice, nasty, or all of the above?

Thanks to fashion's traditional twice-yearly seasonal changeovers – where new looks are wheeled out and pitted against one another in the cluster of various fashion weeks – there's a demand on designers, or on the fashion houses named after them, to churn out the 'next big thing'. In this sense it's not unlike the clapping game where you sit in a circle and, when your turn comes, you have to say a word or phrase related to a certain topic, but mustn't repeat what the other players have said. As the beat falls on you, you must name a new colour or animal, say, or be disqualified. To take the analogy further, the fluffiness, scaliness, toxicity or stinkiness of the animal doesn't matter at all, the only thing that matters is that you come up with a new one.

Following this notion of arbitrariness and forced production, we have Roland Barthes' book, *The Fashion System* (1967), which aims to explain how fashion produces novelty, and then sells it to us as a 'naturally' good idea. Barthes finds historical support for his thinking in the work of Alfred Kroeber and Jane Richardson who, in 1940, made a study of fashion in terms of the measurements of its basic forms

– skirt lengths, sleeve widths, waist heights, etc. – in relation to the temporality of its changes. They came to believe that fashion forms change according to an internal fashion logic, a logic of inversion, which decrees that after wide skirts one wears narrow ones and vice versa, and that with a wide skirt one requires a narrow waist, whilst a narrow skirt means a broader waist, which in turn demands narrow sleeves, and so on. A complete cycle took one hundred years, meaning that clothes worn at the half-century mid-point would, according to the system's logic, be formal opposites of those worn fifty years before. We might very loosely trace this rationale through the enormous panniers of Marie-Antoinette (1780s), to the simple column dress

The Coronation Robes of Sophia Magdalena, 1772

of Madame Récamier (1800), back out again to the billowing dresses of Monet's *Women in the Garden* (1866), in at the ankles for Edwardian hobble skirts (1914), and out again with Dior's New Look (1947). Of course, as we've said elsewhere, you can't reduce the whole of fashion to a single logic, but it's undeniably true that inversion is very important.

Barthes, looking solely at 'the written garment' (i.e. the text that accompanies – or occasionally stands in lieu of – a visual representation of fashion) finds that it employs two strategies in order to deliver fashion to us. He divides written outfits into two groups – A and B ensembles. A ensembles make equivalences between the garment and the world: 'prints are winning at the races', 'the latest fake fur lambswool to fend off the winter chill', 'the Aviator; essential air

Portrait of Madame Récamier by Jacques-Louis David (1800)

Women in the Garden by Claude Monet (1866)

The legendary Dior Bar Jacket from Dior's
New Look Collection (1947)

wear'. Meanwhile B ensembles put forward descriptions of outfits whose unspoken message is that the outfit is fashionable at the time of publication: 'a true Chinese tunic, flat and slit', 'jackets that are outsize and fleecy'. The intended result of the first method is that the fashion signs be naturalised. By aligning the garments with functions or activities it aims to make the clothes appear necessary, or at least allows them a point of entry into the world beyond the magazine. But this method relies on its proximity with the second approach, which just tyrannically states that *this is fashionable*. According to Barthes, systems of meaning work better when they appear to be made up of elements that 'just are': a dog is called a 'dog' because it just is. Likewise each fashion must signify fashion because it just does. If the magazine merely used the first method – where a garment's fashionability is justified by its use or context – then fashion would never change, and would therefore cease to exist, because the equivalences made would never have cause to be undone. If the statement 'these shoes were made for walking' wasn't also imbued with the message 'these shoes are currently fashionable', then the shoes would continue to be made for walking until they wore out, which would be a serious obstacle to selling you a new pair, or seven, in the meantime. We have to be made to agree that this style of walking shoe, and no other, signifies fashion *right now* in order for the system to operate effectively.

This brings about a situation whereby a fashion magazine's primary function is to re-enforce the laws that make its own existence possible. Barthes tells us: 'It is in direct proportion to its very arbitrariness that fashion develops an entire rhetoric of Law and Fact, all the more imperative because the arbitrariness it must rationalise or naturalise remains unchecked.' Because fashion sets up a situation whereby, for now, *that* (state or situation) must only be signified by *this* (garment) it has to use any means within its power to make the relation between the two appear inevitable. When the difference between what is fashionable and what it unfashionable may be decided by something as slight and potentially socially meaningless as a pocket shape or method of fastening, fashion writers must assume firm strategies in order to make these differences appear fraught with significance. However, it is here that fashion runs into a contradiction which risks bringing about its own demise; namely that, at the same time as it needs to make clear the utter seriousness of its edicts, it must also, for the sake of its own self-preservation, make some sort of appeal to common sense – a common sense which states that fashion is fundamentally unnecessary. If fashion takes itself too seriously, then nobody else will be able to (again, see *Zoolander*) so it has to find a way to combine a 'sensible' outlook on its own pronouncements at the same time as upholding them as absolute imperatives. These two necessities combine to form a rhetoric which, according to Barthes, 'is sometimes sublime' due to its apparently unproblematic fusion of contradictory forces. As Barthes points out, this union of high value and worthlessness echoes quite precisely the way in which the women who wear fashion have traditionally been perceived.

Barthes argues for the exact opposite of the causal explanations of the less critical costume historians who conflate 'fashion' with 'what people wore at the time'. While their interpretive method supposes that a particular situation in the world brings with it a mode of dress, Barthes' theory proposes that the garment arrives in a form dictated by its own unimpeachable laws and has to be introduced to the world, either by being shown to have a function, which may be purely symbolic – as in A ensembles – or by being temporarily given the task of denoting 'fashion', and therefore being desirable – as in B ensembles. These two strategies aspire to blend harmoniously. However, A and B ensembles, in their frantic combined effort to guarantee each fashion a happy landing, seem to have much in common with dream-wishes as exemplified in Freud's broken kettle joke: A man defending himself against his neighbour's accusation that he broke his kettle claims that he gave it back in perfect condition, that it had a hole in it already, and that anyhow, he had never borrowed it. The coexistence of differing justifications which, despite having the same goal, have contrasting ways of attaining it, seems to Barthes to suggest that fashion is trying to gloss over something irrational in its own workings.

But what has all this got to do with beauty and ugliness? Perhaps instead of the word 'arbitrariness' here we could insert the word 'omnivorousness'. Each time a new season demands a new set of sartorial ideas designers just have to do their best to cough up. If their ideas are rubbish, this fact will be quite visible, hence fashion designers' well-known tendencies to burn out and melt down. Alexander McQueen (in *McQueen*), Raf Simons (in *Dior and I*) and Isaac Mizrahi (in *Unzipped*) have all appeared in feature length documentaries showing something of the creative pressures fashion designers find themselves under in the run-up to a show. Each of them reaches the outer edges of their sanity, and in the case of Simons and Mizrahi, we're only seeing them through one season. Big designers have to go through this horror twice a year – and that's without the add-ins of dumb things like interim 'cruise collections'. They have to produce something feasibly 'new' at the same time as giving buyers what they want, a contradictory demand which unsurprisingly causes psychic tumult. Mizrahi gets lost somewhere between *Nanook of the North* and the various colours of ice cream, and Simons starts talking about the artist Stirling Ruby with an extreme reverence that makes him seem slightly delusional. But rather than trying frantically to double-guess what other people will like they could perhaps have lightened their load by conceding to Barthes' idea that people can be persuaded to like pretty much anything if it's presented to them in the right way.

One of the many binary-melting aspects of fashion is its capacity to confound any fixed notion of ugliness or beauty. For Veblen, among others, this is one of its failings – a sign of its misplaced values. But you might just as well argue that fashion's omnivorousness is one of its highest virtues. What often gets forgotten when people are haranguing the fashion industry for its persecutory ideals is that fashion also celebrates the abject, the freakish, the excluded and even the underwhelming.

Cynics might suggest that fashion has to do this for a number of unscrupulous reasons. Its insistence on novelty might require it to cast its net wide. Then again, the need for publicity and notoriety might induce people to use shock tactics to arouse attention. In your need to mark your products out as different from other people's you might instrumentalise diverse body types or cultural associations without much concern for the actual people who will continue to be disadvantaged or othered once your interest in them has flittered elsewhere. You might do a rote bit of virtue signalling once in a while in an attempt to persuade people that fashion isn't as bad as all that. This is all awful and undeniably goes on, but another way of looking at it might be to say that the logic of fashion is such that what is elevated today must be denigrated tomorrow and vice versa. Therefore there can never be any fixed idea of beauty, nor of good taste. Everything will come and go. Whatever is currently considered the height of elegance already contains within itself the crass and the shameful. The things we now choose to distance ourselves from might soon be the very thing we rush headlong towards.

There is a famous quote about comedy: comedy equals tragedy plus time. It's attributed to numerous people; Mark Twain, Woody Allen, Carol Burnett. No matter how awful something is, one day you will be able to joke about it. You'll pass through a strange, internal process that will change the value of events for you, so you can stop crying and start laughing. It's also an idea you see in fashion: beauty equals ugliness plus time. No matter how hideous a particular style of clothing might seem, it can be elevated to desirable status. Then later it will become tragic again and you can joke about it. For example, we have seen Christopher Kane's Crocs, Celine's fluffy slippers or Gucci's Deirdre Barlow glasses.

A model wears Gucci spectacles inspired by *Coronation Street* character Deirdre Barlow

It's a well-practised trick – to take the most denigrated thing and redeem it. I've just given mainstream, high fashion examples, but obviously it can happen just as cunningly beyond that world, on people who are very sartorially literate and not at all rich. It might involve doing something to transform the horrible item, or it might be a case of resuscitating it at just the right time. It's a bit like keeping a straight face in a game of poker so that everybody thinks you have brilliant cards. Pool sliders can go from being crappy to brilliant but, as with gambling, you have to time it cleverly and do it with conviction. As Barthes says, you might want to suggest that these shoes are great on holiday, but it would also be wise to make it clear that one must simply don pool sliders post-haste.

The advantage of setting a precedent for finding beauty and desirability in unlikely places is that you actually make it come true. Whereas a moment ago we mentioned virtue signalling as a possible weaselly motive behind fashion's supposed 'inclusiveness', here we are talking about transformation in a more alchemical sense. If you spend £275 on a pair of Bottega Veneta pool sliders, I'm guessing it's not because you feel sorry for pool sliders. Rather it's because fashion's all-consuming indiscriminateness has truly enabled you to discover beauty in this simple, apparently utilitarian object. And if it can do this to a pool slider it can do it to anything or anyone.

Of course, if we're arguing here for a kinder, more

responsible future for fashion, seducing people into buying overpriced slabs of freshly molded rubber is clearly not the way forward. The point would be to take seriously the aesthetic omnivorousness of fashion and to say, yes, it really is the case that all clothes, objects and people can be beautiful. Lizzo is on the cover of *Vogue* because she is a gorgeous woman. Joan Didion was used to advertise Celine for that very same reason. Winnie Harlow's loveliness requires no special pleading. Vintage workwear looks great and sits well on a multitude of bodies. DHL have a sexy logo. Who doesn't love a Wellington boot? We're not talking about a half-hearted diversity scheme, but a genuine decolonisation of our closets. The radical potential of fashion is to include the excluded, to idealise the supposedly non-ideal, and to actually mean it. It's not an act of pity, it's a very real shift in perspective. And rather than throwing the thing out of the window after its season in the sun, perhaps we sometimes even consider it fully transformed. Once fashion has opened our eyes to the beauty of Crocs, say, they can never quite go back to being the joke they once were.

And, while we're on the subject of fashion's 'niceness', it seems only responsible to point out that there is a very real counterpart to the 'fashion meanie' – the 'fashion sweetheart', who is just as ubiquitous in the fashion world, if not more so. Looking at purely circumstantial evidence (aka my friends) it seems that the fashion industry draws in highly empathic, sociable people, who love to work in groups and to be part of a cultural phenomenon that is just as likely to be super-inclusive as exclusive.

Perhaps, before long, we will get to a point where we no longer need a giant, greedy industry to force fashion on us via billboards, swanky store fronts, pop-up ads and so on. We will just produce it ourselves. Charity shops, resale websites and even our own ward-robes, contain more than enough vestimentary beauty and variation to last us well into the future. Thank you, Big Fashion, for giving us all this amazing stuff, and for teaching us to enjoy it. Now here's your carriage clock, please go away and leave us in peace.

– Time: Why We Like to Wear the Same Stuff at the Same Time –

Nowness is a quality much valued in fashion commentary, so much so that there's a fashion and culture channel with that very name. What we call 'now' is also a paradoxical zone in which one may experience pure presence at the same time as running up against the fact that it doesn't exactly exist – 'now' is just a non-space between the present and the past. In order to be truly exciting, apparently, fashion must give form to this infinitessimally minuscule gap. It has to mark 'nowness' by giving it a look, and the history of fashion stands as testament to the fact that it has consistently pulled off this unlikely feat.

Although fashion histories are full of stories of fabulous originary events, these can only be pointed out *post hoc*. Amelia Bloomer put on her eponymous pants and, once everyone stopped laughing, 'bloomers' became a thing. But if women hadn't got behind bloomers in large enough numbers then they would simply have been one woman's pair of supremely large knickers. As I am probably repeating, it's the repetition that makes fashion fashion, not the thing that's repeated. All of which makes it like a signature. To borrow words from Derrida: 'In order to function,

American newspaper editor, women's rights and temperance
advocate Amelia Bloomer

that is in order to be legible, a signature must have a repeatable, iterable, imitable form: it must be able to detach itself from the present and singular intention of its production.' In order to demonstrate that you agree to this contract/exchange of money/marriage your signature in this instance must look like your signature in other instances, otherwise how would we know it was really you? The problem with this is that it opens the way to forgery; if a person's signature has to be roughly the same every time in order to do its job, then it can also be learnt and copied by someone else. So the thing that was designed to prove you were there is the very thing that does nothing of the sort.

In *The Painter of Modern Life* Baudelaire, too, refers to the signature as 'the few letters which can so easily be forged, that compose a name.' Fashion must be infinitely reproducible *now* in order to qualify as fashion. So in order to signify this 'now' now, fashion will necessarily also be able to signify it in future as 'then'. Like writing, it is characterised by 'a disruption of presence'. If every age leaves its signature in the form of fashion, this mark, through which the present announces itself as *here*, at the same time, is capable of telling us that the present *was there*.

As the French philosopher Philippe Lacoue-Labarthe so neatly puts it: 'Nothing happens in the absence of repetition.' For anything to *be*, or to be perceived to be, it must be representable (i.e. imitable and transformable). Which may explain, in part, Baudelaire's conviction that a close observation of fashion returns you to the present and the present to you. Something exciting seems to happen in the present, thanks to the multiple echoes of fashion.

Subjective Time

Putting everything we have so far together, perhaps we have the idea of a symptom and a system. By bringing in one last bit of Lacanian theory, we might then have something to say about the dynamic relationship between the two: fashion as a symptom being worked through a system.

Lacan's two theories themselves aren't overtly concerned with fashion. The one we've already discussed (the mirror phase) is largely about identification, and the one we are about to get onto (the prisoners' dilemma) is about subjectivity and time – although both theories are as far-reaching as you want them to be and can be used to talk about anything from politics to empathy to murder.

Lacanian psychoanalysts are particularly interested in time, in particular the distinction between linear/clock time and subjective time. The length of sessions is dictated by what's being said, rather than by the standardised fifty-minute hour. Time is also obviously important in fashion. You have the twice yearly major seasonal shifts, but also the larger timescale of revivals, rememberings and forgettings that might take place across decades or even, with designers like J. W. Anderson, Alessandro Michele or John Galliano, over centuries. The first rhythm is managed in linear/industrial time, but the second is more subjective.

Open Door Policy

Lacan's prisoners' dilemma is a classic logical problem. Three prisoners are invited to play a game and the winner will be released from jail. They are shown five discs, two black and three white. They are told that each of them will have one of these discs attached to their backs, and the remaining two will be hidden. The prisoners will be able to see each other's discs but not their own – and there definitely won't be any reflective surfaces in the room. The first person to work out correctly the colour of their own disc will be freed. (And they will be asked to explain how they worked it out, to make sure they haven't just guessed.) The discs are placed on the prisoners' backs and, after a pause, the prisoners all begin to move towards the exit together, hesitating from time to time before continuing. Why would they do that? And how can we work out from their weird actions what colours their discs are? To cut straight to the solution, their discs are all white – the two black discs are out of the game. So each of the prisoners can see two white discs on their colleagues' backs. They know that if their own disc was black, each of the others would be seeing a black and a white. If each of them were seeing a black and a white they would be able to tell with absolute certainty that their own disc was white, because if it was black too, the one person with the white disc would be running straight for the door. So if everyone appears equally uncertain about their own colour it must mean that they are all white. But it can't be worked out using pure mathematics as it could have if there were two blacks and a white. The correct solution relies on the equal uncertainty and hesitation of each member. In other words, it relies on time and subjectivity, not just numbers. It's the pause and the confusion that open the path to the correct solution.

For Lacan the solution is divided into three time zones. You have the instant of the gaze, followed by the time for understanding and then the moment of concluding. This makes it very different to an ordinary mathematical problem, which presumes simultaneity. Lacan uses it to speak about the kinds of subjective change that might come about in the course of an analysis, where a person speaks in front of another person and then wonders what that person hears in their speech. It's that kind of uncertain intersubjective calculation that drives the work (the 'controlled para-noia'). It's also a dramatisation of the complex relation between the subject and the external world which, it turns out, isn't exactly external. If you want to know something about yourself, you might need to look at other people. This thing you call 'you' is in fact a series of identifications and imports. Your precious identity relies heavily on external support.

Fashion certainly exhibits this same strange temporality and mutual checking in. It involves paying attention to what other people have got on their backs, and thinking about what they might be seeing on yours. Not to mention the question of whether or not you're 'getting it right'. It's an endlessly interesting, but also sickening, conundrum.

If fashion relies on envy and identification to push it along (literally to keep the industry going), this necessarily introduces problems with time, space and perception. If people have to see something and want it (i.e. to believe it will help them to inhabit their own bodies and lives in some way) they also have to believe that other people will fall for the trick on seeing *them*. Being seen is part of the satisfaction – to become the *object* of envy. The problem is that the better the trick succeeds, say with 'interestingly cut' blue striped shirts in 2015, there will very quickly be too many of them and soon it won't matter if it's a really expensive one from Palmer//Harding or a cheap one from New Look – in either case you risk feeling like just another tragic sheep. Everyone else will have one too, or will already be too cool to have one, and you'll be left behind, a prisoner in your blue striped shirt (which, strangely enough, is what many prisoners wear) and no one whatsoever will envy you. You may want to get through the door first but, in the fashion analogy, you can't answer the question too quickly, and certainly not all by yourself. The correct answer relies on the others. You have to stay in relation.

If it's difficult to give up on the idea of fashion as a big contest, maybe it could become the kind of contest where everybody wins. It seems that fashion, at its most ideal, can be a kind of exciting, social space where everyone's responding to each other – sensitively thinking and interpreting – and everybody gets out of the door at the same time. In other words, perhaps there really can be such a thing as fashion justice.

– Technology: Are Digital Garments
the Answer? –

When in doubt, wear red.
– Bill Blass

I n opposition to 'the false notion the eighteenth century had about ethics', which stated that nature was beautiful and good, while artifice was ugly and bad, Baudelaire insists that in fact 'Nature [. . .] is nothing but the inner voice of self-interest,' and that 'Virtue, on the other hand, is artificial.' And what's more: 'All I have said about nature, as a bad counsellor in matters of ethics, and about reason, as the true power of redemption and reform, can be transferred to the order of beauty. Thus I am led to regard adornment as one of the signs of the primitive nobility of the human soul.' People's capacity to transform their appearance is apparently emblematic of their capacity to correct their intrinsically evil, bestial and criminal constitutions (which is perhaps why Baudelaire refers to the crinoline – which reached new heights of exaggeration in the mid nineteenth century – as 'the principle mark of civilisation'). However, it doesn't follow that Baudelaire believed his fellow urbanites to be the most sophisticated members of humanity. He tells us:

The races that our confused and perverted civilisation so glibly calls savage, with a quite laughable pride and fatuity, appreciate, just as children do, the high spiritual quality of dress. The savage and the infant show their distaste for the real by their naïve delight in bright feathers of different colours, in shimmering fabrics, in the superlative majesty of artificial shapes, thus unconsciously proving the immateriality of their souls.

Baudelaire felt the 'human' aspects of 'human nature' were being threatened by numerous 'highly equivocal nature-lovers'. Somehow modern civilisation had twisted itself into a position whereby 'nature' – meaning everything that people had educated, enlightened and 'civilised' themselves in order to break free from – had somehow, when viewed through the idealising filter of 'culture', been lent a charming, blameless appearance. Perhaps believing that 'savages' were still close enough to the less palatable aspects of nature to see it for what it was, Baudelaire also seems to have felt that they were more appreciative of the benefits of both moral and visual rectification. If 'nature' ceased to be an obvious threat, then 'culture' would lose its exigency, and the world might suddenly seem to be in danger of plummeting straight back into its primordial state of depravity. So Baudelaire's passionate appreciation of the attire of his contemporaries was fired by a firm conviction that what is good in human nature (i.e. not self-interested and bestial) was demonstrated by social institutions such as fashion – which had the double benefit of transforming the actual (or animal) body, and of being a sophisticated collective arrangement, much in the manner of 'virtue'.

Baudelaire was a little lonely in this belief – increasingly so as time passed. By the early part of the twentieth century it appears that almost any forward-thinking intellectual with an interest in science necessarily believed that nudity was the only rational solution to the 'problem' of dress. In Germany there were over a million self-proclaimed 'nudists', all apparently inspired by the notion that undress was the truly modern solution to the problem of clothing.

Flügel and the Historical Drive Toward Nakedness

As we have already mentioned, J. C. Flügel's book, *The Psychology of Clothes,* is one of the most enduring texts in this field, influencing writers on fashion throughout the twentieth century. To be fair, the psychoanalytic aspects of his argument have weathered better than his ideas about clothing reform, but for Flügel these two strands were inextricable.

Flügel begins his book with an outline of what he feels to be the prime motivating forces behind the tendency towards adornment. He states that: 'Clothes serve three main purposes – decoration, modesty and protection.' Apparently 'the primacy of protection as a motive for clothing has few, if any, advocates.' Modesty, on the other hand, 'apart from seeming to enjoy the authority of Biblical tradition, has been given first place by one or two authorities on purely anthropological grounds.' However: 'The great majority of scholars [. . .] have unhesitatingly regarded decoration as the motive that led, in the first place, to the adoption of clothing, and consider that the warmth and modesty-preserving functions of dress, however important they may later on become, were only discovered once the wearing of clothes had become habitual for other reasons.'

In accordance with the sections in *The Painter of Modern Life* that attempt to deal with the decorative preferences of children, Flügel cites a passage from the English psychologist James Sully's *Studies in Childhood* which claims that: '[Young children] like a lot of finery in the shape of a string of beads or daisies for the neck, a feather for the hat, a scrap of brilliantly coloured ribbon or cloth as a bow for the dress and so on.' The child, however, is largely discouraged from giving full reign to this particular partiality: 'While emphasising the need of modesty and protection, we express in various ways our disapproval of the display tendency at an age when it still attaches mostly to the naked body, so that the whole impulse of display is, to some extent, nipped in the bud.' This creates a complex set of relations between the three groups of motives – particularly between those of modesty and decoration. He tells us:

[The] essential purpose of decoration is to beautify the bodily appearance, so as to attract the admiring glances of others [. . . while] the essential purpose of modesty is [. . .] utterly opposed to this. [. . .] Complete simultaneous satisfaction of the two tendencies seems to be a logical impossibility. [. . .] The essential opposition between the two motives of decoration and modesty is [. . .] the most fundamental fact in the whole psychology of clothing. It implies that our attitude towards clothes is ab initio 'ambivalent'.

All of which leads Flügel to conclude that the origination and use of clothes resembles the process involved in the formation of neurotic symptoms: clothes are a compromise solution with respect to two conflicting desires.

Later in his book, Flügel goes on to discuss 'fashion', as opposed to 'clothing'. He believes that people's main reason for wearing fashion is competitiveness and goes on to give an orthodox account of the birth of fashion out of the aristocratic desire for distinction. He does, however, recognise the fact that modern production methods were already making it possible for people to wear affordable versions of more expensive fashions within weeks of their original appearance. However, Flügel finds little to celebrate in all of this. He clearly felt the increased availability of fashionable clothes only encouraged women into ever more dreary narcissistic pursuits, when they might have been better off devoting more time to 'the higher forms alike of work and love and sociality'. His aesthetic sense was firmly rooted in utilitarianism. In opposition to Baudelaire, he was an advocate of the fresh-faced school of beauty and could only see merit in clothes whose design was guided by functionality. He sympathised with members of the many clothing reform groups (with names such as the Sensible Dress Society and the Fashion of the Month League) that sprang up in the early part of the century, whose aim was to make sure people didn't feel bullied by an increasingly powerful media into wearing clothes they didn't feel happy in. He himself was a prominent member of the Men's Dress Reform Party.

Flügel did, however, spot one cheering tendency in the sartorial state of his contemporaries – their greater and greater willingness to flaunt, rather than obscure, their bodies. 'Legs,' he gaily announced, 'have emerged after centuries of shrouding, and adult woman at last frankly admits herself to be a biped. Indeed, in the last year or two, her ankles, calves and knees (all the more dazzling in their suddenly revealed beauty [. . .]) have been her chief erotic weapons.'

Flügel's delight at seeing these newly exhibited limbs seems to have been partly driven by his beliefs concerning the future of dress. He felt that people would do well to try and cure themselves of the 'erotic obsessiveness of nineteenth-century modesty' and it seemed to him that this would involve a relinquishment of the 'compromise solution' that kept this inessential mechanism in place. In other words, he felt that the human race had reached a point in history whereby it ought no longer to need existential support from clothes. Flügel appears to have been partially in agreement with Baudelaire on the topic of the 'primitive' mind. He too thought that 'savages' had a greater need for decoration than modern city dwellers and claimed that more advanced humans tended to be inclined to accept the human body as they found it as opposed to feeling compelled to modify it. In other words, he was more of a traditional racist than Baudelaire. And, like the nineteenth-century nature-lovers who so irritated Baudelaire, you might say Flügel was similarly guilty of believing that the more in control you (imagined you) were of the pervasive terrors of nature, the more enthusiastically you would be able to turn your affections onto your own anodyne fantasy of 'naturalness'. Flügel was firmly convinced that nakedness was the most civilised appearance the human body could adopt, in accordance with 'the general trend of social development,' which, he claimed, 'points to an increasing tolerance of the human body in its natural form and thus an acceptance of "reality".' Trying to pretend to be other than one is seemed immature to Flügel.

More worryingly, he also believed that greater bodily exposure was an effective way to ensure the future survival of humanity. If people would only let other people see the real shapes of their bodies, rather than 'cheating' by using corsetry, padding or high heels, then apparently everyone would be better able to make properly informed sexual choices in order to optimise breeding. Flügel ends his book with the declaration that, in the near future, women will walk around stark naked without anyone batting an eyelid and, moreover, that this will make the human race stronger.

The Emperor's New Pixels

Thankfully, we don't now live in a society where we are coerced by some idiotic idea of naturalism into exposing our naked selves in order that we can be more efficiently appraised as baby-holsters. Instead, we live in a world being not-so-slowly poisoned by the toxic waste produced by the mass manufacture of clothing. However, there is a new alternative to the relentless churning out of physical garments. Non-fungible tokens and digital clothing offer non-physical garments so that we can be impeccably dressed for the metaverse. In 2020 Gucci designed clothes for Sims 4, so your avatar could be supremely stylish while you navigated lockdown in your dressing gown and slippers. Now companies like Dress X and The Fabricant offer NFT wearables and digital garments that can be displayed on your social media. And Instagrammers like @thisoutfitdoesnotexist do a great job of modelling amazing, gravity-defying non-clothes. A rather euphoric article on *The Next Cartel* website gushes: 'No fabric, no waste, right? This is one of the most positive aspects of NFT clothing.' So is that the fashion problem sorted? Stay in, look shabby, but show off endless fabulous sci-fi costumes in virtual space?

Clearly, things aren't so straightforward. For one, embodied life still has an important place in most of our existences. And those of us who are interested in appearing in idealised fantasy outfits online are probably also going to be interested in dressing to impress in real life. If you take pride in your appearance on Tik-Tok, it's likely that you'll want to feel the same when you go out in public. In fact, the more wonderful we look in our digital garms, the more stressed we may feel about honing our real selves better to match our public image. Secondly, digital dressing completely misses the tactile aspect of clothing, which surely forms a very important part of our love of clothes. And thirdly, NFTs are *terrible* for the environment. The first point is pretty well-explored and self-explanatory, but perhaps the second and third could do with a little more attention.

The way clothes feel can make every difference to whether or not we want to wear them. As many of us discovered throughout the pandemic, life is better when you don't have a waistband cutting you across the middle, or shoes that squish your toes into unnatural proximity. More than that, it can feel lovely to wrap yourself up in warm, soft fabrics, or to allow light fabrics to billow against your skin. It's easy to forget about this side of fashion – especially when the focus is on ever-changing styles as opposed to the more general matter of clothing. In fact, this very often gets overlooked by the very producers of fashion themselves, in particular fast fashion. If the only point in a dress is to rush it onto the market as soon after Bella Hadid has worn the 'real' version as possible, then it doesn't matter whether this dress is made from nasty, non-breathable fibres. What counts is a passable visual resemblance. If the dress is only ever going to be worn a couple of times, it can be as sweat-trapping and scratchy as it likes.

If, at the most depressing end of the spectrum, we have the idea of fashion as an uncomfortable spectacle, designed to make us into the best possible visual objects so we can launch ourselves onto the love/work/attention market, then at the other end there is the possibility of privileging the wearer's embodied experience, making our inner experience every bit as important as how we appear from the outside. A good example of this is provided by Issey Miyake, whose clothes not only accommodate the body, using fluid shapes and elastic to allow for fluctuations in weight as well as freedom of movement, but are activated by being worn; they bounce and float, or unfold and refold as you move about in them. Part of the pleasure of putting on his clothes is to feel the ways they move when set in motion.

If there's any doubt about the importance of touch

– in particular, the warmth and softness of fabric – we might remember Harry Harlow's heart-breakingly cruel experiments with macaque monkeys. As part of his research into maternal attachment he placed baby monkeys in cages with two possible 'mothers' – one made of wire, the other from cloth. In some instances the wire mother could provide milk, while in others it was the cloth mother who could feed the baby. What he discovered was that the monkeys overwhelmingly preferred the cloth mother, whether she had milk or not. The babies would take milk from the wire mother but then return to the cloth one, demonstrating that food isn't the only factor in early bonding.

The political scientist, Iris Marion Young, in her 1994 essay 'Women Recovering Our Clothes' argued for the tactility of clothing as a feminist riposte to its male-gaze-pleasing dimensions. Rather than thinking about how our clothes make us look, we might be better off thinking about how they make us feel. By moving towards immaterial garments we would not only be depriving ourselves of a primal, sensual pleasure, but we would be emphasising the visual – perhaps also using filters to make our online avatars into the most idealised versions of ourselves. It's hard to see how this is any route to happiness, although there might be something in it if it were true to say that virtual clothing could help to save the planet . . .

In a sense it's not a complete lie, it just isn't the whole story. While rendering digital garments onto your selfies on Instagram is relatively ecologically harmless, NFTs sold using cryptocurrencies currently rely on outlandish amounts of energy. According to *PC Magazine*: 'a single Bitcoin transaction is estimated to burn 2,292.5 kilowatt hours of electricity, enough to power a typical US household for over 78 days.' So if it seemed at all cool of Gucci and Louis Vuitton to get into the NFT fashion market early, maybe that needs reviewing. Until people work out proper ways to make blockchain technology a great deal less environmentally damaging (i.e. not just by fobbing everyone off with useless, greenwashy offsetting), NFT wearables are not much good to those of us trying to wean ourselves off fashion for climate reasons.

Dolce and Gabbana, in their multo sexy, multo annoying way are all over the very contemporary problem of real versus digital. As Domenico Dolce told a *Vogue* journalist during the launch of their metaverse-themed AW22 collection: 'Instagram only exists if you have a life outside of it.' True, at least for now. The collection was shown on a catwalk that segued from the digital to the corporeal – avatars walked towards the audience on a large screen, and were then replaced by live models wearing the exact same outfits. The clothes themselves were cartoonish in their proportions, with enormous shoulders, bulbous padding and tiny legs. The colours were screen-bright, in fabrics such as shiny red vinyl. The design premise was to produce the kinds of super-exaggerated garments that one

From Dolce and Gabbana's 'metaverse' themed
Autumn/Winter 22 collection

might think could only exist in virtual space. This, of
course, is an amazing technical feat, and probably the
most interesting thing D&G have come up with since
the 90s, but it's a million miles away from the thinking being done by brands like Margiela, Issey Miyake,
Stella McCartney and Vivienne Westwood with regard
to making exciting clothes in the face of ecological
collapse. Instead, the Italian duo chose to celebrate
screen culture using coloured plastics, although they

did make a big song and dance about their 'ecological fake furs' – having only recently agreed to stop using real fur – and to demonstrate effectively that digital clothing is no solution to the destructiveness of fashion as it just creates new aesthetics which ambitious, attention hungry designers then translate into yet more new clothes which will be copied by fast fashion companies, and so on.

In short, between real world nakedness and digital destructiveness, solutions to the fashion problem aren't looking too clever.

– Lucky Punk –

> We were just very ecological about clothes. It was just
> about taking old clothes and wearing them again.
> – David Johansen of the New York Dolls

Environmentalists have a tough time trying to persuade people not to do the things they seem to like doing: flying, driving, consuming animals, buying new clothes. Inside the movement there's a stress on trying to keep things loosely positive in the face of a looming apocalypse. If you make environmentalism sound austere and boring, so the thinking goes, no one will want to join you. But fears about ecocide and societal breakdown don't lend themselves easily to a party atmosphere. Or do they?

One of the sacred texts of my generation is a book called *Please Kill Me: The Uncensored Oral History of Punk*, by Legs McNeil and Gillian McCain. Since I've had it lying around in my kitchen I've lost count of the number of people who've walked in and said: 'That's my favourite book!' It's so seminally cool it's even referenced by Jess in *Gilmore Girls*, which basically makes it unimpeachable. Collaged from a series of live interviews and press cuttings, it tells the story of the birth of punk, between New York and London – how it morphed out of the post-hippie, underground art-music scene into an endlessly influential global sensation. Initially there was no word for the movement; its adherents were just grumpier, poorer and less idealistic than old school, flower power hippies. They'd watched the world fail to develop into a peace-loving paradise and couldn't afford to float from festival to festival without confronting, and feeling compromised by, life's uncomfortable economic realities. Some took heroin in order to experience a sense of release only to find the uncomfortable economic realities of heroin addiction even worse than the standard ones they were trying to slip away from.

In keeping with its subject matter, *Please Kill Me* is an explosion of sometimes conflicting accounts of the same events, one voice sliding into another as a kind of shattered, cubist picture emerges. One of the book's many striking features is the searing, self-reflexive honesty of its subjects. No one gives themselves an easy ride. Everyone doubts their own 'goodness' and 'rightness'. None of them seems to have a plan. As the film director Mary Harron is quoted as saying: 'What was so thrilling about it was that we were moving forward into the future and I had no idea what that future was. I felt like everything was new – there were no definitions, or boundaries, it was just moving forward into the light, it was just the future, everything new, no rules, no nothing, no definitions.'

Hippies had to be good, nice and right, but punks didn't; they also had the option to be bad, horrible and wrong. In the book, there are endless stories about venereal disease, everyone sleeping with everyone else's partner, and injecting heroin with needles filled from puke-laden nightclub toilets. Having said that, an incredibly idealistic philosophy somehow emerges, and it seems to have something to do with honesty. Perhaps it's like the modernist architectural idea of truth to materials: if you are human and, as such, deeply flawed, then this is what you have to work with. Once you stop trying to be marvellous and exemplary you are freer to live a more nuanced, complex and potentially interesting existence.

If this nameless shift involved being somehow different from a hippie, then it also became necessary to *look* different from one. For many of the early proto-punks, like David Johansen of the New York Dolls, this simply meant stopping wearing overtly hippyish clothes without putting too much thought into what you wore instead. Perhaps you wore quite 'normal' clothes. However, you wouldn't go to the shop and kit yourself out in all-new stuff. In keeping with your non-selective, Dadaist outlook (not to mention your poverty) you could just put on whatever was lying around, however tatty, uncool or completely the wrong size. Lou Reed wore plain black T-shirts with jeans, Patti Smith a simple man's shirt, while The Ramones wore classic bikers' leathers.

It wasn't until Malcolm McClaren came to New York and started managing the New York Dolls that clothes became seriously foregrounded. Not content with their slapdash, eco-anti-fashion, he started to dress the Dolls up in matching red leather and vinyl outfits, making them perform in front of a huge red flag. Everyone hated it, including the band, who felt like their new look had nothing to do with who they were. Their friends and fans were confused and offended. What had initially come about organically was suddenly being converted into a product, and everyone hated it.

As the New York Dolls started to fall apart due to drug addiction, bad management and terrible clothes, McClaren began to cast about for the next big thing. The person he admired most in the New York scene was Richard Hell, the singer in a band called Television. In his own words:

I just thought Richard Hell was incredible. [. . .] This was not someone dressed up in red vinyl, wearing bloody orange lips and high heels. Here was a guy all deconstructed, torn down, looking like he'd just crawled out of a drain hole, looking like he was covered in slime, looking like he hadn't slept in years, looking like he hadn't washed in years, and looking like no one gave a fuck about him . . . I don't think there was a safety pin there, though there may have been, but it was certainly a torn and ripped T-shirt. And this look, this image of this guy, this spiky hair, everything about it – there was no question that I'd take it back to London. By being inspired by it, I was going to imitate it and transform it into something more English.

It seems Richard Hell wasn't overly delighted when he discovered a short while later that McClaren was managing a band§ called the Sex Pistols, who dressed in ripped T-shirts, had spiky hair, and sang a song called 'Pretty Vacant' which was all but a paraphrasing of Televison's 'Blank Generation'. Still, he responded philosophically: 'Ideas are free property. I stole shit too.'

From here the rest is tragic fashion history. The Sex Pistols formed in 1975, became famous in 1976,

Punk legend Richard Hell

A safety-pin dress by Zandra Rhodes, 1977

split up in 1978, and lost their bassist, Sid Vicious, to a heroin overdose in 1979. From the diverse, experimental clothing of the early punks – bondage, binbags and tampons for earrings – there developed a quintessential punk style that could be copied by anyone. Pop acts like France's Plastique Bertrand could manufacture ersatz punk hits. In 1977, Zandra Rhodes made the first collection of punk couture – expensive ripped dresses, prettily decorated with safety pins and plug chain. The 'real' punks were not impressed. At least Malcolm McClaren and Vivienne Westwood were actually part of the scene, even if they were simultaneously exploiting it. Rhodes was a prissy purveyor of colourful, floaty silk gowns and had no place appropriating the punk aesthetic, apparently.

By 2013 the influence of punk on high fashion was so ubiquitous that the Metropolitan Museum of Art in New York would host an exhibition called 'Punk: Chaos to Couture', demonstrating over three decades of the appropriation of punk by fashion houses such as Comme des Garçons, Chanel, Moschino, Margiela, Givenchy, Alexander McQueen, Dior, Jean Paul Gaultier, Helmut Lang . . . in short, everyone. Gamely, both Richard Hell and John Lydon provided texts for the accompanying catalogue, neither appearing to have hard feelings. The catalogue juxtaposes pictures of both famous and non-famous early punks, wearing their home-made, idiosyncratic outfits, alongside the high-end copies that have proliferated in the world of couture ever since. The book begins with a classic Chanel suit laced with impeccably crafted moth holes. A McQueen dress made from cling film sits alongside a shot from a 1977 Screamers' gig. A Margiela tank top constructed from smashed plates is shown next to an unnamed man with a spoon on his lapel and a saucer on a chain round his waist. Near the front is a photograph of Richard Hell from around 1976, wearing a twisted and pinned-together shirt that is the very evident precursor of Westwood's 'drunken' tailoring.

What you might deduce from all this is that punk is as cynically commercial as anything else, and that it was pretty much designed that way from the start. But you could also argue that there was something there before McClaren came along to monetise it, and if we could think our way back we might be able to salvage something useful. The premise of pre-commercial punk was to come up with something funny and cheap with whatever you could get your hands on. And you didn't have to spend loads of time on it either. Craft was not cool. The world was falling apart and you didn't have time for fancy embroidery, let alone sewing a button back on. You had to live as though it might all end tomorrow. The nuclear threat, plus economic melt-downs on either side of the Atlantic, made it seem wise to exist in the moment. As Vivienne Westwood says in *Poly Styrene: I Am A Cliché* (a documentary about the legendary X-Ray Spex singer): 'You could just put on your dad's jumper with a pair of black tights and run off down the road'. The funny thing is that this approach to dressing might also turn out to be a good way to preserve the future. The first wave of punk clothing also happened to be environmentally friendly, and it's surely no accident that Vivienne Westwood has since become a major spokesperson for transforming the clothing industry into something more sustainable.

Vintage Schmintage

We are constantly being told these days that vintage and second-hand clothing is the way forward. Well-meaning newspaper articles encourage us to shop on resale websites like Vestiaire Collective, and stars are congratulated for wearing vintage gowns on the red carpet. But apart from the fact that this way of dress-ing can be incredibly expensive, sometimes it simply doesn't appeal to people. For a start, the older amongst us might dread the idea of dressing in the styles of our youth. But what if we rethought what it meant to wear existing clothes rather than buying new stuff?

One of the misconceptions around second-hand clothing is that the people who wear it just happen to like recreating looks from different eras. Maybe they go swing dancing too, or decorate their homes with psychedelic wallpaper. But as punk shows, it's pos-sible to wear old clothes in a futuristic way – it was only when McClaren stopped being obsessed with shiny red textiles that he could finally see a way for-ward. The genius of early punk was that it immediately opened up whole new sets of possibilities that were accessible to absolutely anyone. You could wear tiny clothes, or huge ones. Or tiny clothes over huge ones. You could put things on upside-down or back-to-front, or turn shirts into skirts. You could even wear things that wouldn't normally be considered clothes at all. Once you rejected the idea that your clothes ought to make you look wealthy and conventionally attractive you could start to play with them in new and evolv-ing ways. And the surprising effect of this was it could even make you instantly charismatic. By refusing to be a flunkey to the system, you demonstrated a strength of character that drew other people in. As evidenced by the Met show, everyone wants to be a bit punk.

Now and Zen

Thanks to the wish for a sharp break from hippiedom, there might be a tendency to disavow the importance of Zen Buddhism to punk philosophy. But as soon as you start to look at the history of punk the connection becomes clear. If Andy Warhol and The Velvet Underground form a bridge between the swinging sixties and seventies punk, then they bring with them the associations with the contemporary art and music scene – the composer, John Cage, with his experiments in chance-controlled music, and the choreographer, Merce Cunningham, who used the I Ching to direct dancers' movements. Warhol himself is often characterised as a great businessman who was mainly interested in wealth and celebrity, but this is to miss the enormous emphasis in his work on emptiness, non-judgement, silence and the absence of meaning. The New York music scene that birthed punk was infused with a history dating back to early minimalism, with its links to Eastern philosophy. If you listen a little differently, catchphrases like 'no future' take on a slightly different inflection. Or this quote from Richard Hell: 'We had no attachments, nothing to lose.' Or John Lydon: 'Punk was all about changing – continuously.' It's also surely not by chance that the punk-inspired grunge band Nirvana were called Nirvana. Once you start to look, it's everywhere.

All of which is to say that a re-mining of punk

doesn't mean wearing a mini kilt with a safety pin through your nose. You might end up looking really sensible, like a late 70s David Byrne. The point would be to try to let go of as many persecutory ideals as possible and see what you end up with. What if clothes could be rethought from the ground up? And not just by clothing specialists, but by anyone? Instead of taking the imitable parts of punk, we could take the inimitable bits – the things that happen by chance. Maybe choose an outfit according to comfort and nothing else. Or wear all your favourite things at once. Or dress in the clothes your partner leaves on the floor. Whatever you like. Or don't like. It literally doesn't matter. Here John Lydon gives a perfect example of working with what's under your nose: 'Because of the rubbish strikes in London, there were garbage bags piled twenty high on every street corner. What the council did was that they started putting out bright green and bright pink rubbish bags to kind of gentrify the trash. Well, that was a perfect, perfect item of clothing to a wannabe punk at that time. You'd just cut a hole for your head and your arms and put a belt on and you looked stunning.' Of course, these days, the point wouldn't be to wear a bin bag like you're going to a punk fancy dress party, but to wear whatever appears in front of you that makes you laugh or gives you an inexplicable buzz. Maybe that's your mum's old stuff. Or your kid's. Or the things your neighbours leave on their garden walls. Or a kitchen apron someone gave you although you never cook. If you like it, wear it.

And if this all sounds a bit woo, there's the slightly less radical but highly real-world trick that punks perfected under the guidance of Vivienne Westwood. Perhaps if you go fully out on a limb with your clothes you might risk feeling like a nutter. The reason people seem to like designer brands is that they feel authenticated, or rubber stamped, by expensive clothing; if Demna Gvasalia says it's OK, it must be OK. But there's nothing less cool than going out and buying a fully put-together designer look so what you do is buy one carefully chosen designer piece and then use it to orient or pin down all the other weird shit you wear around it. In Viv Albertine's book, *Clothes, Clothes, Clothes, Music, Music, Music, Boys, Boys, Boys,* she describes visiting Westwood's World's End shop in the mid 70s and being persuaded by Westwood herself to buy an expensive pair of red boots as an investment. The thing about the boots was that they were so purposeful-looking in their own right that you could wear pretty much anything with them and the boots would make it look good. Albertine was cash-strapped but went along with it, and the boots were still going strong when her book came out in 2014.

Maison Margiela is another surprisingly Zen post-punk design house. Founded in 1998 by the Belgian fashion designer Martin Margiela, the brand initially specialised in showing the inner workings of traditional clothes. Every part of the construction and process was liable to be revealed, from chalk marks to tailors' tacking to linings. The 'truth' of the clothing was fully on show. Another house speciality is the 'Replica'; a piece of comically flawed old clothing is lovingly reproduced – maybe a holey jumper, baggy old man's nightshirt, or pair of boots covered with cracked white housepaint. I was lucky enough to stumble across one of these pieces in a second-hand shop, a cream silk blouse that must have gaped between the buttons, so the original owner had added visibly-stitched black poppers at the mid-point between buttonholes. The effect is funny and gauche. The poppers are such a 'bad' solution to the problem of gape that the replicated blouse is a sartorial joke, like a perfect copy of a two-year-old's drawing.

The genius of Maison Margiela (whose clothes are now designed by a huge, diverse team of clothing nerds under the supervison of John Galliano) is that the shop is full of clothes it takes five minutes to make and that look completely brilliant. Their design ethos has a strong environmental bent – they're big on upcycling – and surely so few people can afford the stuff anyhow that their print runs can hardly be enormous. But anyone can walk into the shop, quickly work out that the £590 'Foulard Hat' is simply a man's shirt buttoned around the head and chopped off round the back, then go straight home and get the scissors out. They are also great for ridiculous styling; knotted hankies on the head with HUGE denim jackets and socks

Maison Margiela's 'Foulard Hat'

with sandals, all of which can easily be found on eBay. For eco-inspo, Margiela is great. They are also the best at elevating what already exists to the sweet spot where the abject meets the sublime. Applying the well-worn – and totally Zen – logic of the fine art ready-made (a tradition inaugurated by Marcel Duchamp's urinal), Maison Margiela subverts the unfortunate fashion idea of interminably making people want what they don't have, instead encouraging people to marvel at the kind of stuff they probably already own, or could easily pick up for next to nothing.

To sum up, if you take a look at what punks were up to you discover a number of options:

You can wear whatever the fuck you like.

You can buy one expensive thing and wear it with whatever the fuck you like. (And the expensive thing could even be from eBay.)

You can look at what clever nerds manage to do with abjectly awful garments, and then go home and do it yourself.

– Fashion's Alternative Future –

There are many different futures implicit in the present, some of them a lot less attractive than others.
– Terry Eagleton, *Why Marx Was Right*

T he problem with writing a manifesto is that it involves telling people what to do. If the main point in the manifesto is to tell people not to listen when other people tell them what to do, then that could cause complications. In trying to dismantle an old set of persecutory ideals you might just end up with a new lot: 'Wear whatever you like!' 'Recycle! Sew! Don't shop!' 'Be your own authority!' Instead of curing the disease you just recast the symptoms. But this is not that sort of manifesto. It's a new, non-bossy kind that offers multiple suggestions and leaves it up to the reader to do what they like. (Except binge on fast fashion, obviously – totally not allowed . . .)

The thing about fashion is that it's already brilliant. Or at least it contains within itself the capacity to be brilliant if you are selective about where you place the emphasis. Instead of emphasising the need to be rich and conventionally beautiful we might tune in to fashion's love of the grotesque and bizarre. Or its capacity to disrupt hierarchies. Or its celebration of the mundane. Or its admiration for resourcefulness. Or its batty capriciousness. Once you de-emphasise the idea that it's a conspiracy of wealthy (and would-be wealthy) villains to make you relentlessly dissatisfied so that they can con you out of money, then you can get on with enjoying it.

In Terry Eagleton's book *Why Marx Was Right* he attempts to debunk the main Marx-bashing myths: 'Communism is horrible, just look at Soviet Russia.' 'Marxists are obsessed with a class system that no longer exists.' 'Revolutionary politics involves violence.' 'Everyone loves to live in liberal democracies – even the ones who whinge about it (and who are actually allowed to, thanks to the marvellous liberalism).' And, for the purposes of this book: 'Socialists are naïve about human nature; humans are inherently aggressive, rivalrous and competitive.' Eagleton doesn't disagree with the idea that people are troublesome, but he points out that certain cultural conditions breed certain sorts of trouble. If you live in a dog-eat-dog world, you'd better get out there and eat some dogs. But in so doing, you'll always be afraid of being eaten yourself. However, if you develop a taste for vegan dog pellets – and especially if you can convince other dogs to do likewise – you can maybe start to relax a little. Not all of your problems will be solved, but at least you'll be able to walk down the street without constantly looking over your shoulder.

It would be simple-minded to imagine that fashion can swiftly and smoothly transition into a perfectly just and socially responsible system. However, it already has enough beneficent qualities to help train it a little further in that direction. The people who like it and wear it just need to stay on track and remember, as far as possible, not to be dickheads. That way we will find it ever easier to be comfortable in whatever we choose to wear. Nothing needs to change *that much*. That's the upside of this particular manifesto – it's in praise of what's already there. Not just the actual clothes, waiting out there in charity shops and on resale websites, but in fashion's entire methodology.

Of course, manifestos need to be succinct and well-organised, otherwise they're just rambling diatribes. So, finally, here's a list of the things we need to bear in mind if we want to keep enjoying fashion as we hurtle into our uncertain future.

Fashion is a Conversation with the World

Like any good conversation, it needs to find a rhythm between speaking and listening. Sometimes the world will tell you something and you can sit back and hear it. Other times you might really have something you need to get off your chest, in which case maybe trust the world to be able to take it. If that means wearing latex socks with gladiator sandals, so be it. It's perfectly possible to wear such things in the spirit of 'anything goes', as opposed to the spirit of: 'I hope no one will hate me too much for this,' or: 'I'll smash those normie fuckers to smithereens with my devastating avant-apocalyptic footwear.' You have no idea what the world will think, so just talc your feet, sock-up and see where it gets you. Same goes for a twinset and pearls.

Men, Women, Whatever

Wearing a twinset may differently impact the conversation according to whether you're male, female, non-binary, cis or trans. It's easy enough for an inner-city cis woman to be all heroic about what a person can get away with wearing, but I don't want anyone to get beaten up. Still, the conversation around clothes and gender is moving fast and let's hope it's only a matter of time before the arbitrary dress codes that dictate who can wear what completely collapse. In Chiara Cremin's *Man-Made Woman* – a book that coins the term 'criss-cross dressing' – we are told: 'By dressing in women's clothes, I stand apart from the world as it is and embody an idea of a world that ought to be, a world that is to come. In such a world, clothing is an expression of individual style with no correspondence either to sex or gender, words that become meaningless.' This is the world I would like to live in and I'll stand by anyone who wants to help us get there. If you meet someone who actually believes there's something natural or inevitable about super-binarised dress standards, just direct them towards some seventeenth-century portraiture, or Sumerian skirts.

Insist that Your Clothes be on Good Terms with Your Body

Never be at war with your own clothing. I say this as a person who knows a great deal about holding onto too-small clothes 'just in case'. Fuck that. Our clothes need to be nice to us, not besiege and torment us. Also, the fact that Tik-Tok has completely decommissioned fusty fashion HQs such as *Vogue* means that there are no more formal diktats about what to wear when. No longer can there be a scenario whereby this season requires miniskirts but, oh no, you have thick legs. For one, skirt length is between you and your skirt. For two, all legs are beautiful. For readers of Flügel, eugenics is just bad science. Anyone in any doubt just needs to read Angela Saini's excellent book, *Superior: The Return of Race Science.* 'Good legs' are not a thing.

Further than that, it's important never to lose sight of the fact that clothes can feel nice. If 'nice' to you means bound and laced to the point of fainting, I salute you. Equally, if it means hunting down vintage cashmere, or buying clothes a size or two bigger than your mum thinks is correct, go you. While humans continue to inhabit real space and time, your clothes should be on your side, helping you to do that.

Take a Good Look at Yourself

Don't be embarrassed about enjoying the alienating effect of unfamiliar outfits. If it gives you a buzz to look in the mirror while trying out some new clothing arrangement, that's brilliant. It doesn't mean you're a tragic narcissist. It means you're using your weirdly structured human psyche to get temporary pleasure from self-misrecognition. Given that we're doomed to look outwards in an endless quest to understand what goes on inside us, maybe it's a good idea to get some kicks along the way. If you see someone who you think looks amazing – perhaps someone who looks particularly 'themselves' in their clothes – what better way to pay tribute than to see how it feels to put on something similar yourself? Does some of your admiration for them rub off a little on you? Great! It's OK to like yourself. Someone might even see you looking and feeling a bit good about yourself, which might in turn help them. Rivalry isn't the only social relation. Copying can be kind.

If It's Out, It's In

There's no such thing as bad taste. I'm not referring to the snotty idea that 'proper' aesthetes know how to include something a little off-kilter in their otherwise impeccable visual universes. I'm saying fashion teaches us that anything and everything can be beautiful. Yes, it has a tendency to do it in a pesky way; if something's been considered beautiful for too long it might have to spend a few years in the dog house. Still, we all know it'll be out again before we know it.

In my home we have a game. Think of a garment or style that's so ridiculous or uncool that the very thought of wearing it makes you laugh. Tell someone else in the house about it. See the look of incredulity on the other person's face when you say it will be the next big thing. Ruffs, bonnets, drop-crotch trousers, Laura Ashley sailor dresses, steampunk, whatever. Then wait a couple of months before victoriously shoving a picture of it under their nose, maybe in the latest *Hunger* magazine, on Carey Mulligan, or in the new Gucci campaign. You will always win this game. Especially if you bought said thing on eBay before the prices went up.

There is no item of clothing that's off-limits to fashion. In fact, the more off-limits it seems, the more fashion heat comes off it. It doesn't even need to be ugly, outrageous or stupid. At home, when playing 'the game', we have sometimes experimented with more even-tempered fashion concepts. For example, in late 2020, while we were in lockdown, we joked about the possibility of Breton tops and sailor clothes becoming ultra-cool. How could it be done? They were so Boden, so middle-classly ever-present; the last place you would ever look for inspo. And lo and behold it happened; the first post-pandemic stroll down New

Bond Street revealed a Miu Miu window full of naval collars, and an article in spring *Vogue* pressed home the importance of dressing like Proust on a seaside break.

The Future of Fashion Might Look Silly at First

In time, one hopes, big shops and glossy magazines will recede so far as to be an unnecessary part of all this. As people wean themselves off Big Fashion they will be able simply to vibe off each other without the authenticating presence of a powerful fashion Other. (I know this will never happen: Miu Miu will have swanky stores until the end of days . . .)

Whatever kind of clothing you would instinctively say 'no' to, just say 'yes' instead. Not only will this make you and your loved ones cackle furiously, it will give you the mysterious charisma of Baudelaire's passer-by. 'What is it about that person?' the promenading poets will ask. And the response will be that you answered the call of fashion's future in the affirmative, blindly, faithfully, in the knowledge that the world will eventually agree with you, even if it takes a month or two to catch up.

No Red Vinyl

Not only did this material almost cause the demise of the New York Dolls, it was also a notable feature of the 2022 Dolce and Gabanna 'Metaverse' show. I rest my case.

The Death of the Author is Real (Unless the Author is You)

Fashion comes out of nowhere. Of course it has a history. Yes, it's a system. For sure it's an industry. But it's also a mess. Some people take it as axiomatic that everything you read in *The Devil Wears Prada* is true. However, the famous bit where Miranda Priestly kicks off about the sanctimonious narrator's determinedly unfashionable jumper, tersely explaining that she and her fashion homies dictate all trends, ever, and that moreover, thanks to the trickle-down effect, this means they are personally responsible for the look of absolutely all clothes, is wrong. Even before the advent of Tik-Tok it was delusional to believe that fashion was set by an inner clique of botoxed autocrats. As we've seen, there are many differing stories about where and how fashions originate: from the fluctuating styles of defensive aristocrats, to the inspired leaps of original influencers such as Amelia Bloomer, to the artistic authority of individual designers, to the machinations of faceless capitalists, right up to the anarchy of social media platforms. You simply can't say which of these is true – they all are. Which also means they all aren't, or at least that you can't rely on any one of them to trump the others. The fashion editors of this world might go all out to impose their limited vision on us, but there are more things in heaven and earth, Miranda, than are dreamt of in your magazine.

Fashion is More Like a Potato than a Pyramid

Rather than trying to trace each style or garment back to a pure, original moment, it's more sensible to concede that fashion's underlying structure is rhizomatic. And that it always has been – it's not like those aristos were plucking novel ideas out of the ether: some of them were copying milkmaids. There's never been a proper, top-down hierarchy: people have always nicked good outfit ideas from somewhere. Therefore we might as well agree that there's no higher fashion authority than *you*. Designers such as John Galliano are on the record as saying that they basically get ideas from looking at crazy grannies. And Shein might be mass producing one of your Depop items as we speak. Perhaps there are people who like the idea that there's an actual puppet-master in charge of all this, but thinking that Anna Wintour is the boss of everything is about as sensible as going along with QAnon. (This is basically the plot of *Zoolander 2*, in case you were too high-minded to go and see it.)

Challenge Everything

The other day, one of my neighbours set out to under-stand the style of the local youth. 'It's like they're try-ing to demonstrate that they haven't made choices,' he said. 'They look like they've put their clothes together at random. Each garment is awful and it doesn't go with the other ones. Is that the point?' (This neighbour is always dressed head-to-toe in the kind of wholesome clothes that appear in ads on the *Guardian* website.) I'd never have thought of it quite that way, but I think I see what he was trying to get at. These people are certainly giving a look to the present but it isn't yet easy to define what that look *is*.

A counterpoint to this would be walking down the street with my twenty-something kid, who might sometimes say: 'That person looks cool.' I used to have to pause for a minute to work out why they'd said it. It would never be a person I'd have flagged up as well-dressed. It made me curious. What was it about this person that my kid was responding to? A pattern emerged. The person was making absolutely no concessions to the kind of annoying style or beauty standards that my 1950s mum had tried to instil in me. (I don't blame her: I think she just has a highly self-critical inner voice that spills over onto the people she cares about.) They didn't look all 'put together'. They definitely hadn't spun around in front of the mirror and taken one thing off, ffs. They were certainly not all thin. Or pimple-free. Or tidy. Or even young, for that matter. They just looked naturally odd, as if – to borrow from Lady Gaga – they happened to be born that way. They hadn't done anything in particular to make themselves look weird; they seemed somehow constitutionally characterful. They definitely wouldn't be wearing new clothes (except maybe trainers) but neither would their clothes look fastidiously vintage. They wore things that seemed to require a certain amount of courage and wit, but were quite different in each case. They might or might not be wearing make-up but if they were, it probably wouldn't involve contouring and highlights (except when it did). They generally wouldn't be hyperbolising the supposed features of their biological gender (except when they were). They looked like people with interesting interior lives; people who it would be fun to talk to.

Once you broke it down you could see that these individuals really were deeply cool. As I understand it, they are truly rethinking clothes. And they are taking everything into account. They are problematising gender norms, and questioning ideals around wealth and beauty. Plus they are doing it in an ecologically sound way. They are also perplexing to older people – at least ones without twenty-something translators to hand – as, for now at least, they don't have a style that can be named, copied and sold back to them. I know Urban Outfitters are probably trying, but if anything these kids probably shop in kilo stores, where clothes are sold by weight. These shops are great because they're full of the exact items that no-one has quite recognised the value of; basically all the stuff the fussy vintage dealers don't want. In a sense it's the most amazing negative sorting process. By putting all the least cherished garments in one place you inadvertently generate an unnameable style. Of course this makes it just like that other moment in the mid 1970s when something similar started to happen, but perhaps this time we will be wiser about the commodification of peculiar clothing.

So that's it. Let your clothes be chatty and comfortable, whatever comfort means to you. Affirm your own sartorial sovereignty. Challenge everything. Even the red vinyl rule, if you think you've found a way to do it with spirit. The future of fashion is already in your wardrobe. It's not just that fashion contains the potential for change within itself, but that the revolution is already underway.

ACKNOWLEDGEMENTS

Thank you first of all to Rosalind Porter at Notting Hill Editions for letting me write a book on my favourite subject. Also to everyone else at NHE for making the book exist, and Melissa Chevin for telling people about it. Very special thanks to Tracey Cahoon for organising the cover shoot, and for being such a brilliant friend. Also to Michèle Côté and Polly Banks for the photos, clothes and really fun meetings, and Anna Inglis Hall for make-up, Hannah Burton for assisting and Beatrice-Rose Brierly for modelling. As ever, thanks to Devorah Baum, Josh Appignanesi, Chloe Aridjis, Darian Leader, Ren Brown-Martin, Ajay and Ninder Khandelwal, Heather Johns, my yoga teachers, the people who deliver my eBay packages, Peter and Roslyn Grose, Dot Grose Forrester for being a razor-sharp interlocutor, and Robert Brewer Young for being such a generous first reader.